When Demons Are Not Under the Rock

Amy Karen Downey

IHP PRACTICA

Paperback ISBN: 979-8-9990929-6-0
Hardcover ISBN: 979-8-9990929-7-7

IHP PRACTICA
An Imprint of Illative House Press, LLC
500 E. Elm St.
West Frankfort, IL 62896
IllativeHousePress.com

Scripture quotations in this work are taken from the King James Version, public domain. Emphases added are the author's.

Cover design: Illative House Press and Amy Karen Downey

All IHP publications are available through Amazon.com.

ILLATIVE
HOUSE

PRESS

Praise for *When Demons Are Not Under the Rock*

Dr. Amy Downey has taken a complicated, scary, and confusing aspect of the Christian life and described it in ways everyone, from all walks of life, can understand. Not only that, Amy provides practical examples on how spiritual warfare impacts everyday life as people try to walk with Jesus. Her personal stories, exegesis, and application, make this readable for everyone, from the Seminary Professor to the new believer.

Pastor John Seferian, Craigville Bible Church, Chester, NY

In the world of blame and poor spiritual doctrine concerning spiritual warfare, this book is both a refreshing breath of pure doctrinal air and compelling counsel for the reader. Every person must deal with spiritual warfare. The believer isn't called to spend his time looking under every rock for a demon or the devil, but spiritual warfare is a reality in the life and struggle of those who choose to follow Christ. Realization and recognition of this battle and the Biblical principles for 'battling' are desperately needed. So much can be gleaned and implemented in a person's personal spiritual life and the warfare he fights from the chapters and teachings of this great book, *When Demons Are Not Under the Rock*. I would urge you to make this part of your 'boot camp' experience in preparing for the spiritual warfare you will face as you follow Jesus.

Dr. Dennis Parish, Executive Director, Lone Star Pastor Care Network, Conroe, TX

With wisdom, courage, and biblical clarity, Amy Downey opens a much-needed conversation in *When Demons Are Not Under the Rock*. Her use of Scripture, combined with vulnerable personal reflections and focused study questions, draws the reader back to truth and provides a thoughtful framework for engaging with Scripture on this often-overlooked topic.

E. Burnett, Missionary to Restricted Access Nations

When Demons Are Not Under the Rock is a raw, honest, and deeply biblical look at the spiritual battles believers face when the struggle feels unrelenting and unseen. Drawing from powerful scriptural narratives—especially the life of Jeremiah—this book reminds us that spiritual warfare isn't always loud or obvious, but often found in seasons of grief, isolation, and obedience. With pastoral wisdom and practical truth (as she was a pastor's kid after all), it guides readers to persevere, trust, and find God even when the darkness feels overwhelming. A timely and necessary resource for anyone walking through the trenches of faith.

Pastor Mark Haney, Harvest Fellowship Church, Leedey, OK

Amy Downey's *When Demons Are Not Under the Rock* gives a more Biblically accurate view of spiritual warfare in that most of the battle is with-in ourselves and how we deal with situations beyond our control. It has helped me take a fresh look at discouragement, sacrifices that must be made in ministry to the Lord, and staying true to God's word when the enemy is making real and personally harmful attempts to silence that truth.

Pastor Michael Sims, Bayside Community Church, Valdez, AK

Dedication

Jack Henry Downey was my first best friend,
and he will be my daddy forever,
even though he left this world on 4 July 2000
– his ultimate Independence Day.

He held my hand while I prayed to receive Jesus as my Savior and Messiah.
He choked up as he baptized me, his daughter, and his sister in the faith.
He (and mama) took the discipleship of their daughters seriously and allowed
us to grow, make mistakes, and find our way even while
praying fervently for us behind the scenes.

However, and most of all, I do not know of anyone who lived out their faith
with more grace and kindness than this man, known by only a few
but who changed the lives of so many.

I want to be Jack Henry Downey when I finally grow up.

Foreword

When I met Dr. Amy Downey, her mother, Barbara, and I had met as two new teachers at an elementary school in Texas. I had remarried and moved to the area, where I found a job at the school. Barbara was a pastor's widow and had moved to get a fresh start. As our friendship grew, I was introduced to her two daughters.

It wasn't long until I understood the spiritual influence that these two daughters had been raised under. Amy's dad had been a minister until his death, and Barbara had been right beside him, fellowshipping and providing the duties of a pastor's wife. Additionally, I was told many stories about the girls' early years – how they were instructed in God's word and, at a young age, both of them felt the call to serve the Lord in ministry.

When I met Amy, she was teaching history at a Baptist university in Arlington, Texas. However, I wondered why she wasn't also teaching Biblical studies, given her extensive knowledge of the subject. I wasn't one to question. But I marveled at Amy's knowledge of the Gospel and her intelligence in interpreting Scripture. I was 30-plus years her senior, yet she possessed a remarkable gift of understanding the Bible and its meaning to people.

However, it was not long after I met her that she decided to begin her work on her PhD studies at Liberty University while also maintaining her work as president/missionary of Tzedakah Ministries (which started in 2004). She took the leap of faith, which meant leaving teaching, for she knew that while we are not promised an easy road, we are promised that God will sustain us.

I watched her grow in faith, knowledge, and compassion. Her desire to understand the Jewish faith and its beliefs propelled her to delve deeper into the biblical text. I was impressed by her ability to interpret the Bible and Jewish doctrines and her ability to hold in-depth conversations with many "learned" scholars. She was also tenacious and stood her ground backed in Scripture and with love.

I wish I could say that Amy's journey has been smooth sailing, but it was not. She has been tested at every turn. Many do not want a "woman" expounding on the word of God or calling out leaders who do not always have their faiths or agendas in line with Scripture, nor did she float through her doctoral program. She supported herself, worked in her ministry, and paid her own way through school. I remember times she sacrificed her own needs to use her funds to carry out her ministry. She graduated with high honors at Liberty University (2016) while she faced the fiery darts of Satan, who attacked her at every opportunity.

When Dr. Amy Downey sent me a copy of her third published book, *Paul's Conundrum*, I was amazed by her insight and depth of Paul's ministry. I have read about Paul many times in my Bible studies over the years, but I was captivated by the deeper knowledge and foresight Amy had of Paul's work. I honestly could not put it down. I must also confess I had to call her and ask several questions about some of the information and how she was able to understand it, let alone explain it. As a teacher, Amy knew that a student cannot grasp knowledge until they are led to it. Her ability to bring the text into layman's terms gave me a new "Aha" moment of "I never thought of that like that."

Amy's second book, *Missions in the Minor Key,* explores the minor prophets, their works, and their insights. Again, Amy has taken such deep spiritual teachings to light their meanings and applications. Her ability to interweave her own personal experiences in the book brings these prophets to life in real situations, giving us closer, more meaningful comparisons to our own lives. Now Amy has brought us her latest in-depth study, *When the Demons Are Not Under the Rock* – a look into how spiritual warfare can be a component of discipleship that should not be overlooked.

Dr. Amy has led us through many avenues of study that are biblically documented and divinely inspired through her writings. I know this book will inform and uplift the reader in finding a closer walk with the Lord in their studies, prayers, and relationship with our Messiah.

Mrs. Judy McCord
Midlothian, TX

Author's Preface

Prefaces are not the easiest part of a book to write. One is always afraid that one is going to leave someone out who is very important to one's life or include someone that years later you regret including. Trust me ... that has happened!

When I wrote *Missions in the Minor Key,* I thanked three amazing teachers who had a profound impact on my life, and I must do so again – Virginia Dailey, Ketta Casey, and C. Barnwell Anderson. Mrs. Dailey and Mrs. Casey were not afraid of this uber-nerd and her penchant for asking odd questions at the most inopportune times. And ... I will never forget Mrs. Dailey's grace for allowing me to have a Big Red while waiting for my daddy to pick me up on my first day of first grade. Professor Anderson from Jacksonville College was a history professor beyond grace and knowledge. He could have gone anywhere and been recognized for the brilliant man that he was. However, he chose to remain at a small college in East Texas, where I was transfixed every day by his lectures and gentle wisdom.

When I studied at Southwestern Baptist Theological Seminary and Liberty University, the men and women who crossed my path were some of the luminaries in their fields. To name them all would ensure that I omitted someone important to my life, but I must name John Morrison, who just passed away (2025), and Leo Percer at Liberty, and as always, James Leo Garrett, Jr., and Calvin Miller at Southwestern. Four individuals who lived and live out their passion for Messiah Jesus in a way that personifies grace and kindness.

As you will discover as you delve further into this book, my parents were, and still are, the most influential people in my life. To say that they were and are my heroes is an understatement. I wish everyone could have met them, for they are the most amazing people I have ever known. My sister and I have often acknowledged that while they were not perfect – they overcame so much to give us lives defined by unconditional love.

I wrote this same paragraph in *Missions in the Minor Key,* and I will write it again. I always have to remember Josef, Agnes, William, Rosalie, Suzanne, Jack, and Vera. These names in isolation might not mean much to anyone. However, to me, they mean the world as they are seven people who survived the Holocaust and whom I was able to call my friends. They have all died now, but I am the bearer of their history, both before, during, and after the war. I know who they lost and what they went through during the Shoah. I love them all and I know who I believe I will see again in Heaven and those who never came to faith in Jesus, and to quote one of them – "would rather go to hell with their family who died in the camps than go to Heaven without them." They all had heard the Gospel of Jesus, yet my heart and soul still hurts at the thought of…

As a missionary to the Jewish people, every breath I take is about sharing the Gospel to one of God's Chosen People. I exist to be a missionary. I battle another day so that a Jewish soul might have a chance to know that Jesus is their Messiah. For "salvation is from the Jews" (John 4:22).

Amy Karen Downey, Ph.D.
tzedakahministries.org

Table of Contents

Part One: Spiritual Warfare – When Does It Begin for a Believer?

Back in the late 1990s, before I became a missionary to the Jewish people, I was the "Spiritual Life Coordinator" at Jacksonville College, located in the small East Texas town of Jacksonville. Any attempt to explain my title, however, is complicated because, as a woman, I was not allowed to have the title of Campus Pastor or Campus Minister. Still, my actions would often reflect what those roles entailed – including counseling a young freshman woman who had her favorite animal die while she was away from her home for the first time. To put it simply, I was essentially the equivalent of a BSM Director for Southern Baptists or the campus leader of organizations such as CRU, Navigators, or any other college Christian organization you can imagine.

And while Jacksonville College was affiliated with the Baptist Missionary Association of Texas (and briefly with the Southern Baptists of Texas Convention), many students on campus simply needed Jesus — including some of those considered the "good kids" on campus. I seemingly had the impossible task of bringing the message of Jesus to what was considered a "Christian campus," but I did my best.

We had a Monday night campus-wide Bible study and a Thursday night Bible study in the Women's Dorm. We hosted a Backyard Bible Club for the children in the community, and I sought to raise awareness of the truth of Matthew 25 on campus through Coats for Kids and Canned Food Drives. We even had a group from the college choir sing for the local homeless shelter while I was there, and those good-hearted college students were, for lack of a better word, traumatized to discover there were homeless people in a town of 12,000 people. And for a multitude of reasons, I am still trying to forget the drama caused by the 1997 Harvest Fest (aka Halloween Carnival) hosted by the college for local community children, because good Christians do not celebrate such a night!

Thankfully, several college students came to faith during my time at Jacksonville College, and a few went on to full-time service as pastors, missionaries, and others. Students who are now parents of their own, and with whom I still have contact in various social media venues. They have grown in their faith, grown in their emotional maturity, and have even grown up enough as adults to now call me ... "Amy."

As I walked some of those same students through the decision of coming to faith in Messiah Jesus, I always stopped them before they made the final decision and asked them a simple question — **"Are you SURE you want to make this decision for Jesus?"**

1

Now ... this might sound like a weird question for a "Spiritual Life Coordinator" to ask, but you have to understand the reason why I asked them this question. Yes — heaven is at the end of the journey. Yes — hell is the primary goal that one wants to avoid for all eternity. **BUT** ... the Christian life is not a bed of roses for anyone. **BUT** ... a true follower of Jesus does not have it easy in this journey we call life. And so, I wanted to know if they were prepared for the journey they were about to embark upon as they "said the salvation prayer." Incidentally, you should know something about me: I never did a repeat-after-me prayer with those college students ... and I still do not in my role as a missionary to the Jewish people.

For as I followed up on that first question, I explained my question with an important follow-up statement —

> *If you say YES, you will make the absolute worst enemy of your life. His name is Satan, who will do everything in his power to make your life miserable. He will want to hurt you because he no longer has control over your eternity. He will be angry and want to destroy your joy. HOWEVER, and if you say, YES ... you will also have made your best friend who will be by your side and ready to fight for you and with you. You just have to ask. His name is JESUS. Are you SURE?*

Interestingly, and this is important for you to know as you begin this book, I never had one single person turn down the opportunity to receive Jesus as their Messiah. They all decided that it was better to have the best friend named Jesus in their corner and that it was more important to have him, even if it meant acquiring the worst enemy named Satan. They decided Jesus was a better decision, and I am glad they did.

However, I thought it was important for them to know what I am about to tell you. Spiritual Warfare, I believe, begins for a Christian, a believer in Messiah Jesus, the moment you become one. Spiritual warfare is more than the movies and other books make it out to be, and I hope this simple effort will help you to be prepared for the battle that does not simply lie ahead but is with us now every day and every moment of our lives.

1

Spiritual Warfare Is Often Always a Good Thing
(Joshua 5:13-15; 1:6-9)

We are sometimes asked to fight a battle alone in the world of spiritual warfare, with no answers regarding the outcome, because we are standing on holy ground, and we are fighting this battle for a holy cause.

I know that when many Christian people of a certain age hear the two words "spiritual warfare," their minds will often return to those classic or infamous (depending on your literary viewpoint) works by Frank Peretti — THIS PRESENT DARKNESS (1986) and his sequel PIERCING THE DARKNESS (1988). However, and regardless of your perspective of Peretti's predictable approach to Christian fiction. I do know a phenomenon began in the Christian world with these books, as it seemed that everyone started to look for a demon under every rock, and the words "spiritual warfare" were falling from everyone's lips.

Obviously, I am not a huge fan of Peretti's works (and I did read them), but please know that I do believe that the spiritual world is darker and far more dangerous than most Christians recognize. I do believe that "the forces of darkness" do seek to destroy the Christian witness at every opportunity available. I do believe that Christians need to be careful in the paths we trod and what we expose ourselves to in this world (i.e., movies we watch, books we read, music to which we listen).

However, I do not believe we should be looking for demons to fight or that we should be looking for those demons who may or may not be under every rock. Why? Those demons do not need us to come looking for them, as they will come looking for us! And as a missionary to the Jewish people, I can and will provide examples throughout this book of when I have encountered spiritual darkness in the heavenly realms. But ... I did not have to go looking for them because they were and are ready to battle for me and you every minute of every day.

Instead, I believe the real spiritual warfare that we engage in every day life is one designed for our strengthening. Yes, you read me right ... *Spiritual Warfare IS a Good Thing!* **A perfect example of this truth can be found in the life and times of Barney Fife. Yes ... that Barney Fife of "The Andy Griffith Show" that our grandparents watched when they were young and can even now be found on reruns on Nickelodeon and other networks sometimes. Yes ... that Barney Fife who was on TV when television was still black and white, and dare I say when television was still funny and safe and clean.**

Barney was bumbling, stumbling, and a bit of a doofus, but he was always willing to go towards the battle/crime even when terrified because he learned something about himself and the law every time he went. He also became just a little bit braver with every experience. This can be true in the development of spiritual warfare for us in our Christian life as well.

My favorite episode of *The Andy Griffith Show* perfectly captures this truth and concept. In "Lawman Barney," Barney Fife sees two area farmers breaking a local ordinance by having a vegetable stand inside the city limits. At the beginning of the episode, he confronts them rightfully but without any power and with a great deal of fear masked by false bravado. They run him off from the vegetable stand, and in turn, he feels like a coward and a failure. The remainder of the episode is a series of events in which Barney discovers that true power is not within himself but in the badge he wears (i.e., the law).

In the closing scene, he confronts the farmers again, but with the power of the badge as his weapon, because he is no longer fighting them alone, as he has grown through the experience. He has discovered he is standing on ground that others have already fought over before him and the ground he has under him is rock solid. By the way ... remember that thought in the next few pages and as we go throughout this chapter.

This is what we as believers in Jesus should remember as well. We must go through a spiritual warfare of development at times when we feel like cowards and failures and "Fifian" doofuses more than once along the way. But those often painful experiences are good things as they teach us something very important – self-reliance is not a good thing.

Here is another spiritual lesson we can also learn from Barney Fife – we should also have only one bullet to shoot off in our gun – but we will get to that idea later because it is time to get to the Scripture idea!

Joshua 15:13-15 – Fighting the Battle Even When You Receive No Answer

A few years ago, my Bible time took me to Joshua 5:13-15. Joshua 5 is the passage following the circumcision of the Israelites (ouch!) after they failed to do so during their forty years in the Wilderness and before the Battle of Jericho in Joshua 6. Joshua seemingly is off wandering alone when he encounters God in what we in those nerdy, theological circles call a "Theophany" – a pre-incarnate visit with Jesus.

And it came to pass, when Joshua was by Jericho, that he lifted up his eyes and looked, and, behold, there stood a man over against him with his sword drawn in his hand: and Joshua went unto him, and said unto him, Art thou for us, or for our adversaries? And he said, <u>Nay; but as captain of the host of</u>

the *Lord* am I now come. And Joshua fell on his face to the earth, and did worship, and said unto him, What saith my Lord unto his servant? And the captain of the *Lord*'s host said unto Joshua, Loose thy shoe from off thy foot; for the place whereon thou standest is holy. And Joshua did so. (Joshua 15:13-15)

Joshua asks a basic question in today's language that would boil down to simply — "Are you for us or against us?" as his focus is on the battle ahead and what is seemingly impossible in human standards, taking down the impenetrable walled city of Jericho. He does not receive the answer to his question, but he does receive a command — "Take off/Loose/Remove your shoes for you are standing on holy ground."

I can only imagine that Joshua was thinking to himself while he took off his shoes — "Are we going to win? My soldiers are hurting back there from a rather uncomfortable medical/spiritual procedure. And … I am scared." However, did you notice that Joshua was never given based on the passage itself the answer to his question — **"Are you for us or against us?" He was commanded to do what Joshua did, for the verb is in the imperative tense, which is a command in Hebrew, which is to remove his sandals because the ground was holy.**

I have been where Joshua was at that moment (thankfully, minus the circumcision because I am, after all, a female), and I am sure you have been there as well … many times. But what I was told was my own version of — "Take off your shoes for you are standing on holy ground." And if you are like me, you want to say … **"BUT … COULD YOU ANSWER MY QUESTION FIRST ALREADY?"** However, the only answer I am given is, "Take off your shoes for you are standing on holy ground."

> *This is the ultimate test of spiritual warfare! DO YOU/I TRUST HIM OR NOT?* "SOMETIMES WE ARE TO FIGHT AN INDIVIDUAL BATTLE IN THE WORLD OF SPIRITUAL WARFARE WITH NO ANSWERS REGARDING THE OUTCOME BECAUSE WE ARE STANDING ON HOLY GROUND (DOING IT FOR A HOLY CAUSE)…"

This was what I wrote in my journal the morning I had my Bible time in Joshua and this was the test that Joshua had to face because he had to take off those shoes and obey because Joshua 6:2 — which is the promise of victory — had not yet been promised to Joshua. And sometimes Joshua 6:2 is not promised to us either … and sometimes it is never promised at all. And it is during those times that we have to decide -- do we trust the Captain of the Lord of Hosts enough to take off our shoes?

This reality of trusting God when we either receive no answer or the answer that we humanly do not want is a tougher battle in the spiritual warfare campaign than any demon might throw at us, because it involves trust. This is a tougher battle in the spiritual warfare campaign of the Christian life because it consists in believing even when the circumstances seem impossible. This is a tougher battle in the spiritual warfare campaign because we might lose a momentary battle, but we have to trust the General who has our best spiritual interests at heart. Yes, Spiritual Warfare is a Good Thing ... even when we are scared to death (and even when we feel like Barney Fife and not Joshua) because we have to walk on "Holy Ground" with no shoes on.

Joshua 1:1-9 – Be Strong and Courageous ... Period

Perhaps you wish I had started with this passage instead of Joshua 15:13-15, for Joshua 1:9 is often listed as people's life verse and can be found on wall plaques in Hobby Lobby. And, indeed, verse nine in this passage is an affirming and encouraging verse for every believer in God to hold onto when the day seems dark and the night long. However, it must be read in the biblical context and in light of the biblical setting in which it was given to gain a full understanding of its power. This passage needs to be understood beyond the tapestry and/or coffee mug that it is found today, or its only purpose is to be a decorative wall hanging or a cup to keep cocoa warm on a winter's day.

This is the reason I started this chapter with the second passage because the courage to engage in the fight of spiritual warfare cannot be found in a bookmark found in the pages of our Bible, but has to be found within ourselves and our relationship with God ... even if we do not know the outcome. With this truth understood, we can now discuss the biblical principle of courage correctly.

> Now after the death of Moses the servant of the Lord it came to pass, that the Lord spake unto Joshua the son of Nun, Moses' minister, saying, Moses my servant is dead; now therefore arise, go over this Jordan, thou, and all this people, unto the land which I do give to them, even to the children of Israel. Every place that the sole of your foot shall tread upon, that have I given unto you, as I said unto Moses. From the wilderness and this Lebanon even unto the great river, the river Euphrates, all the land of the Hittites, and unto the great sea toward the going down of the sun, shall be your coast. There shall not any man be able to stand before thee all the days of thy life: as I was with Moses, so I will be with thee: I will not fail thee, nor forsake thee. <u>Be strong and of a good courage:</u> for unto this people shalt thou divide for an inheritance the land, which I sware unto their fathers to give

them. <u>Only be thou strong and very courageous,</u> that thou mayest observe to do according to all the law, which Moses my servant commanded thee: turn not from it to the right hand or to the left, that thou mayest prosper withersoever thou goest. This book of the law shall not depart out of thy mouth; but thou shalt meditate therein day and night, that thou mayest observe to do according to all that is written therein: for then thou shalt make thy way prosperous, and then thou shalt have good success. Have not I commanded thee? <u>Be strong and of a good courage;</u> be not afraid, neither be thou dismayed: for the Lord thy God is with thee whithersoever thou goest. (Joshua 1:1-9)

As a stepping stone to explaining the passage, I would like to share with you that Harry S Truman is my all-time favorite president for several reasons. One of the primary reasons is that despite pressure to do otherwise from the U.S. State Department and his own Secretary of State, George Marshall, he immediately recognized the modern state of Israel only eleven minutes after the official declaration of Israel by the nation's first Prime Minister, David Ben-Gurion, on 14 May 1948.[1] Truman also stepped into enormous shoes as he became the 33rd president after the death of Franklin Delano Roosevelt on 12 April 1945. He had only been the vice president for a few weeks, and the country was still in the midst of World War II, even though the war in Europe was rapidly coming to an end as the Allies approached the outskirts of Berlin.

However, Truman was tasked with leading the world in closing out the war in the Pacific, and there seemed to be no quick end in sight. For he had no clue on April 12th about the secret weapon that was being developed in Los Alamos, New Mexico, when he took the presidential oath after FDR's shocking but inevitable death.[2] The president was faced with a series of impossible

---

[1] Clifton Truman Daniel, "First Family Stories," Truman Library Institute, available online at **https://www.trumanlibraryinstitute.org/israel/**; accessed 19 November 2024. See also, "Key Press Release on the Recognition of the State of Israel." *Social Education* 42, 6 (October 1978): 469; available online at **https://www.archives.gov/education/lessons/us-israel#background**; accessed 19 November 2024.

[2] History.com Editors, "President Truman Is Briefed on the Manhattan Project," available online at **https://www.history.com/this-day-in-history/truman-is-briefed-on-manhattan-project**; accessed 19 November 2024. Actually, it was almost two weeks after he became president before he was introduced to the reality of the Manhattan Project.

choices – unleash the first "Weapon of Mass Destruction" on the world or invade Japan and anticipate millions of American soldiers to be killed or injured in the midst of the invasion (and additional millions of Japanese citizens).[3] Therefore, Truman chose to drop the first nuclear weapon in warfare on 6 August 1945, and World War II ended a few days later, but the consequences of that decision live with us even today. Truman faced those choices and lived with those choices because, as he always said, "the buck stopped with him."

I shared that rather lengthy introduction of my favorite president, for President Truman, in some ways reflects a person who had to step into another impossible situation … Joshua. Can you imagine the pressure of following Moses? The man who led the people out of Egypt. The man who had led them through the Red Sea, led them through the Wilderness, led them for almost forty years, was gone, and now it was up to his "understudy" to take on the mantle of leadership and take them the rest of the way home … but a home the people of God had never seen. Talk about pressure. Talk about an emotional and spiritual level of warfare for someone to take on. Reminds me of the 1981 song by David Bowie and the band Queen, for Joshua must have felt as if he was definitely "Under Pressure" even to attempt to follow Moses, but lead the people he must.

The first four verses of the passage inform us that Joshua was once again given his command orders and the promise that the Israelite people would be victorious because God was with them. As we consider verse 5b, we are allowed to see that the words are specifically a promise to Joshua that God will not fail/release/let go of Joshua, nor will he abandon/forsake, or leave Joshua behind. These promises from God had to be such a weight off of Joshua's shoulders because I am certain that Moses' understudy felt millions of pairs of eyes on him and were just waiting to say to him, "Moses wouldn't have done it this way." Yes, Joshua was under a great deal of pressure.

This is why God told him three separate times in verses 6-9 to be strong and courageous. Yet, we only seem to focus on verse nine and not the first two times in which God makes the land possession promise to Joshua and the command to follow the Torah/Law. And I would point out now that following, meditating, and not turning away from the Word of God is what I believe to be as a living embodiment of Barney's single bullet (see I told you we would return to Barney Fife and the Mayberry Police Department).

---

[3] "Harry Truman's Decision to Use the Atomic Bomb," National Park Service, available online at **https://www.nps.gov/articles/trumanatomicbomb.htm**; accessed 19 November 2024. I had three great-uncles who were active in the military at the time, and they were all informed that if an invasion were to occur, to anticipate a 50% casualty rate.

For we can only truly be strong and courageous when we are armed with the Scripture firmly established in our hearts. We can only truly never be alone (v. 9) when we have devoted ourselves to meditation and pushing ourselves forward in the study of God's promises – which is the idea of prospering found in verse 8. We can only truly overcome our fears and discouragement and avoid falling prey to the attacks of spiritual warfare when we are armed with the only bullet that Barney Fife (and ourselves) ever needed – the Word of God, deeply invested within us.

Questions for Individual or Group Study

1.   Without giving in to the tendency to give a "Sunday School Answer," what is your human response to the idea – **"We are sometimes to fight a battle alone in the world of spiritual warfare with no answers regarding the outcome because we are standing on holy ground and we are doing it for a holy cause?"**

2.   Why do you think God so often chooses not to provide the answer to the questions that we ask, especially when we are in the midst of a spiritual battle?

3.   What do you think of the argument that "spiritual warfare is a good thing" and that it is for spiritual development? Where do you agree with this argument? Where do you disagree with it?

4.   Have you ever fallen victim to the "Bible Verse Tapestry" approach in that you claim a verse as a promise without understanding the background and context of the passage? Why do you think that Christians are so prone to this approach to Bible reading today?

5.   How can we use this chapter as a foundation to see that spiritual warfare is not about demonic warfare but about growing in our walk with God on a daily basis?

2

Spiritual Warfare Is Often Always a Thorny Issue
(2 Corinthians 12:1-10)

We often have to recognize that the first battle in spiritual warfare is with the one that we fight within ourselves. The battle that we fight to release one's personal ambitions and dreams in order to achieve God's better plans for us. This is perhaps the most challenging and enduring battle of them all.

I remember the sermon. I remember where I was sitting in the Baptist church in the small country church – fourth row back on the right side, because the piano was on the right side for some bizarre reason, according to Baptist perception. I remember the internal reaction I had in my mind, my heart, my soul when God's words reached my heart. I remember every moment as if it were yesterday instead of almost forty years ago. For while on the surface, I was a goody-two-shoes pastor's kid, underneath, I was in open rebellion against what God was telling me to do with my life.

The sermon my dad was preaching that Sunday evening at Moorewood Baptist Church in Leedey, Oklahoma, was from 2 Corinthians 12:1-10, and the verses are etched into my brain, my heart, and soul – much like the branding irons that were used on cattle that roamed across the Western Oklahoma prairie hills not far from the church –

> And lest I should be exalted above measure through the abundance of the revelations, there was given to me a thorn in the flesh, the messenger of Satan to buffet me, lest I should be exalted above measure. For this thing I besought the Lord thrice, that it might depart from me. And he said unto me, <u>My grace is sufficient for thee: for my strength is made perfect in weakness.</u> Most gladly therefore will I rather glory in my infirmities, that the power of Christ may rest upon me. Therefore I take pleasure in infirmities, in reproaches, in necessities, in persecutions, in distresses for Christ's sake: <u>for when I am weak, then am I strong.</u> (2 Corinthians 12:7-10)

It was not enough that God already knew that this 16-year-old teenage girl did not like the idea of being vulnerable and weak. He was also asking me to turn over complete control of my life, my dreams, and my goals to him. As I looked at those verses and heard my daddy's sermon, God revealed His plan for my life. A plan I wanted nothing to do with because it was not my plan … not my plan at all.

Now … I have to admit that God did not unveil every moment of my life to the 16-year-old Amy, or I might have run out of that small Baptist church and run across those same prairie hills where the cows were and headed for Kansas looking for Oz or anywhere else to go. No, God only gave the barest of outlines, but that was enough to begin a rebellion in my heart and an ongoing effort to negotiate with the King of the Universe that did not end until I was twenty-nine, when I finally gave up to His purposes. By the way, it is never a good idea to try to negotiate with the creator of the world because you lose every single time.

What God revealed to me that night, along with these verses, was that I was going to be a missionary, and that my dreams of being a wife and a mother would have to be put aside, as He had different plans for my life. I was being called to a life of singleness – even if I did not have the gift of singleness – for this reality was going to be my thorn in the flesh for the rest of my life. And I must confess that, even now, almost forty years later, I am writing this sentence with tears in my eyes, for being a wife and a mother (and now a grandmother) was something I have never stopped wanting.

For we must begin to realize that spiritual warfare sometimes starts within ourselves and is sometimes the greatest battle that we are asked to fight. A battle that will not be fought just once but will be fought over and over again in our lives. Paul understood this truth, and his vulnerability in sharing this unique, spiritual encounter with God is why we need to examine this text more closely and more often. Yet it is a text that still bothers me when I read it – even forty years later.

2 Corinthians 12:1-10 – Thorns Hurt … Regardless

Of all the Brontë sisters, the least well-known is likely the youngest of the three, but perhaps the most religious of the sisters, Anne.[4] Charlotte is known for one of my all-time favorite novels, *Jane Eyre*, as I adore the love story of Mr. Rochester and the governess. Emily wrote the equally well-known *Wuthering Heights* with the brooding Heathcliff and the spoiled Catherine. Anne wrote two lesser-known novels, but it is for poetry that she is perhaps the most recognized. One of her poems, "The Narrow Way," features a beautiful stanza

---

[4] "Anne Brontë, Universal Salvation, and the Narrow Way," available online at **https://www.annebronte.org/2018/09/02/anne-bronte-universal-salvation-and-the-narrow-way/**; accessed 22 November 2024. The blog writer argues that Anne became convinced of the argument that ultimately God will relent and allow people to be saved from eternal damnation. I do not know enough about Anne's life to make an argument either for or against this view. Regardless, the view itself is incorrect, and I can only hope that she did not hold to it.

that perfectly illustrates the overall concept of spiritual warfare, which I aim to convey through these verses.

On all her breezes borne,
Earth yields no scents like those;
But he that dares not grasp the thorn
Should never crave the rose.

One online analysis of the poem argues that the poet "presents a stark and challenging perspective on the path to spiritual fulfillment."[5] Perhaps the analyst also would consider the "path to spiritual fulfillment" to be the final and eternal fulfillment that occurs at death. However, the path of spiritual warfare and/or spiritual maturation/development could still be true here. For I believe that we must all be willing to grasp the thorn that God places in our path for personal growth if we ever want to smell the roses at the end of the road of life.

Therefore, and as we consider the significance of Paul's thorn in 2 Corinthians –regardless of what it might be,[6] I think it is important to recognize the idea and/or definition of the thorn itself. I remember that my own daddy proposed that the identity of the thorn was left purposely vague so that we could see our own deficiency or weakness in these verses. I wonder if that was Paul's intention, but I understand why my dad would see this as the rationale for Paul's vagueness. For you see, my dad was born in 1934 with what is today called a cleft palate, but in less Politically Correct times was called a hair lip.

In 1934, my grandparents were wonderful but simple tenant farmers during the height of the Great Depression. Expending the funds to repair their son's facial deformity was something that most people could not have imagined doing; however, they did what they could because Henry and Gladys Downey were amazing individuals. The doctor who performed the surgery was not a plastic surgeon but a simple country doctor who did what he could, both times, as the first surgery tore after only a few weeks. Ultimately, my father's upper lip was never centered with his nose, and there was a scar from a doctor who did his best in a time that was torn apart and depressed for the whole country.

---

[5] Analysis of "The Narrow Way," available online at **https://allpoetry.com/The-Narrow-Way**; accessed 22 November 2024.

[6] J. W. MacGorman and Frank Stagg, NT consulting editors, *2 Corinthians-Philemon* (vol. 11), The Broadman Bible Commentary (Nashville, TN: Broadman Press, 1971), 72. Speculation on the specificity of the thorn runs the gamut from eye disease, epilepsy, effects from malaria, ongoing guilt from his days as a persecutor of Christians, and even fighting an ongoing temptation of the mind or heart.

My sweet daddy always struggled with a sense of self-worth from the small scar on his face even though the woman who loved him for all the years they were married, and even the twenty years she waited to join him again in Heaven, never saw it and only saw her knight in shining armor. My sister and I only saw a daddy who let them walk on his feet when we were little and knew his arms would always protect us regardless of how old we were. Yet, his scar was his thorn because he saw himself as disfigured, and I believe he wondered if this held him back in his service to God. And that is one personal reason why I believe it is so important that we understand what Paul meant by the word itself – thorn – for we all have scars. Some are visible, like my dad's, and some are invisible to the world, but they all shape us in ways that few recognize or understand.

The word that Paul used for thorn, skolop in Greek, is a combination of two words – *skello* (leanness) and *optanomai* (gaze and/or inspection; related to the eye). This is perhaps why some believe Paul had an eye issue; however, let me propose an alternative for all of us to consider. What if Paul's "thorn in the flesh" was something that the man of God was forced to examine and confront within himself – an internal but spiritual issue or battle that he recognized as a weakness in his walk with God?

Am I engaging in as much "navel-gazing" as others who are seeking to diagnose Paul's thorn in the flesh? Perhaps. However, I am also attempting to find the balance between those who saw Paul's infirmity as a physical or spiritual issue and my dad's interpretation, which allows all of us to see our weaknesses in Paul's place. Yes … I believe there is a place in the text for all the belly lint analyses to be true. See what I did there with my little pun?

James M. Scott, in his commentary on 2 Corinthians, points out that beginning in chapter 10 (and especially in chapter 11), Paul is forced to confront those who challenge his right to call himself an apostle of the Messiah Jesus.[7] Today we would laugh at such a challenge but Paul did have to defend his right to a place on the "apostleship mantle." This is where we find in 2 Cor. 11:22-33 Paul's resume of suffering for the Gospel – the times he was beaten, stoned, shipwrecked, hungry, cold, naked, imprisoned, and all for the sake of the Gospel. Yet Paul felt the need to defend himself, so he began 2 Cor. 12:1 with these words: "It is not expedient for me doubtless to glory. I will come to visions and revelations of the Lord."

In other versions aside from the KJV, the word "glory" is often translated as "boasting," and this is perhaps the best translation in our modern

---

[7] James M. Scott, *2 Corinthians* (vol. 8), New International Bible Commentary, NT ed. W. Ward Gasque (Peabody, MA: Hendrickson Publishers, 1998), 193-221.

understanding. Paul did not want to boast about what had happened to him (v. 2-4) as it applied to "visions and revelations" from God. The actual vision could be his encounter with Jesus on the road to Damascus in Acts 8 or perhaps during his time in a region called Arabia that Paul went to after his spiritual transformation in Damascus (Gal. 1:1-20).

Little is known about the three years in Arabia except by implication in the letter to the Galatian church and specifically what is found in verses 16-18:

> To reveal his Son in me, that I might preach him among the heathen; **immediately I conferred not with flesh and blood**: Neither went I up to Jerusalem to them which were apostles before me; but I went into Arabia, and returned again unto Damascus. **Then after three years,** I went up to Jerusalem to see Peter, and abode with him fifteen days. (emphasis added)

We know from Acts 8 that Paul began preaching but was confronted by opposers and had to be rescued from the city. What happened in Arabia is a matter of speculation and mystery, except for these three verses, but one can guess – he conferred not with flesh and blood but more than likely with the one he encountered on the Damascus Road.[8] I have often described it from my own speculation as Paul spending time at his personal "Jesus Seminary" to learn what he needed to become the great missionary he was destined to become.

One can then understand why Paul was silent about this time in Arabia. How could anyone understand this encounter unless one had a similar encounter themselves? Was this why Paul went to Peter in Jerusalem (Gal. 1:21) when he finally returned and met with the disciples, because Peter was one of the three who encountered the transfigured Messiah before Jesus' death? Perhaps … but we will have to wait until we see Peter and Paul in Heaven to ask. Regardless, Paul's encounter left him with this thorn that was never absent from his side as long as he lived. It truly was the ever-present "thorn in his flesh," and there was a purpose for it.

The idea of a purpose to a painful thorn is difficult to grasp in our current situation, isn't it? This is why I can understand Emily Brontë's poetic lines about not craving the rose unless one is willing to grasp the thorn as well. However, and for me to explain my understanding of this concept, I must share something of my own encounter with God that is hard to explain to others and perhaps difficult to even believe for many.

---

[8] MacGorman and Stagg, *2 Corinthians-Philemon*, 87.

14

A few years ago, I was in Jerusalem on my second trip to Israel. I was staying at the Christ Church Guest House, located within the Old City and close to the Kotel (Western Wall). I walked down to the Western Wall, and while I am not one of those to insert a prayer into the wall as I find that unnecessary and purposeless, I do pray at the Kotel for the salvation of the Jewish people (and I shared a humorous story of my mama's Western Wall prayer in *Missions in the Minor Key* as an example).

On that particular day, I found myself praying more intensely than I had ever prayed before. Before I realized what I was saying, I asked God to give me his eyes for the lost in the world and to help me see the people in the world as he does. Before I knew what was happening, I was sweating and feeling dehydrated. Many might say it was because it was Israel but I was not there during a "hot season of the year." Many might say it was because I was jet-lagged but I was feeling fine just a few minutes earlier. However, I found my way back to the guest house which is near the Jaffa Gate, drank a lot of water, and fell asleep for the next 12 to 16 hours. Yes, I slept for over half a day before I could even attempt to wake up!

And while I had been a missionary to the Jewish people for over ten years by that time, I had never been the same since that prayer at the Western Wall. I truly believe that I now see people with different eyes. My heart for the spiritually lost in the world has grown to the point that there are times when I wonder if I can breathe. However, I still struggle to share this story with you who are reading this book, as I believe Paul did in the first part of 2 Cor. 12, because he did not seek to glory in himself but wanted to give glory to God. How can I show what God did for me without showing myself – and I believe that Paul struggled with this same question.

This, for me at least, is the ultimate question of spiritual warfare, and perhaps why I have struggled so to write this chapter. Paul was given the vision and then the thorn. I was given the thorn and then the vision. However, the battle in whatever order I or you might encounter is all for the purpose of shaping us to reflect God's image and not our own. We do not need demons to shape us—sometimes we just need thorns that God gives us to do it.

As we finish up this chapter, I am perhaps the only one with a few more questions, but maybe you also have a few that you have always wanted to ask but were afraid to voice them aloud. Do not worry … I have always been the one to voice my questions loud enough for everyone to hear. In fact, when I was probably no more than ten years old, I would ask my daddy what it felt like to be "raptured" so many times that he finally told me – "When it happens, I will tell you." Well … that did not satisfy me at all because I then told him, "Daddy, but I will know when you know. Why can't you tell me NOW?"

Isn't this how we feel about many issues in our lives – personal, spiritual, and financial? We want the answers … NOW! If you don't, I can confess that I do. As I read this passage a few years ago, I wrote down a few of the issues in my life, accompanied by the question: "Can we have more than one thorn in our life?" I admit that I struggle with loneliness, but is that tied to the call of singleness and the requirement to be childless in my life? So that is not another thorn but simply an outcropping of the original one.

My greatest fear in life is the fear of failing God because I believe I am so inadequate in life to do what God has called me to do. The massive inferiority complexes of my childhood often come out from their places in the closet or under the bed (i.e., the monsters of our childhood nightmares) to tell me that I am going to fail everyone … especially God … because I am such a horrible missionary. However, is that another thorn or just my flesh resisting the call on my life? This, I believe, is the "messenger of Satan" (v. 7) that is needed on a certain level, for myself at least, to keep me humble so that I will not exalt myself. For while I do struggle with inferiority issues, I also struggle with a sense of self-pride that needs to be kept in check. Do other people have an actual "messenger of Satan?" Perhaps, yes. However, the choice to remove the thorn is not in our hands but in God's alone.

This is the point of verses 9-10. His grace is sufficient and He is strong in our weakness because we have let go. Trust me, I have always struggled with the first part of verse 9. Yet, and for my own sake, I have to be self-weak to be Jesus-strong. And I believe this is the ultimate spiritual warfare lesson for us all in this passage. Sometimes, we are asked to endure horrible circumstances and to let go of our own abilities to receive God's sufficient grace.

Yes, it is humanly hard but externally necessary so that we can be useful for Messiah Jesus. Yes, it is contradictory to American thinking but it is the heart of being Christian-minded. This is what Paul meant by the phrase "so that the power of Christ may rest in me. The word that is often translated as "rest" is *episkenoo* and it literally should be understood as "fix a tent over" or "to dwell upon." If one wants to fight and win this emotional and difficult type of spiritual warfare as found in 2 Cor. 12:1-10, one will ultimately be found enveloped/tented over by Jesus' power. Otherwise, we will only be weak and never strong (v. 10).

When I was in seminary (Southwestern Baptist Theological Seminary), I met a man I will call "Scott." From the moment I met Scott, I was in love. It was not the puppy dog kind of love. It was not the first crush kind of love. It was the deep, forever kind of love that leaves you forever changed. Scott and I just clicked. We laughed at the same jokes. We would talk for hours, and even when we were in the church social group, the rest of the group would just disappear and be forgotten. When you saw Scott, you saw me, and vice versa.

Yes, I knew what God had told me about his calling(s) in my life but I was certain that Scott was going to be the exception to the rule. God was going to give me an out and allow me to have what I always wanted: Scott, children, and a normal life. God was going to relent because I had done my time as a poor pastor's kid who had attended eleven different schools before graduating from high school. And besides all that, daddy liked Scott as well.

Then one summer, Scott left for a youth internship at his home church. We wrote letters all summer and into the fall until one day, the letters just stopped. I would write, but no letters came from Scott. I waited, but only silence from Scott. Eventually, I had to let go of the Scott dream and move on with my life. One day, a few years later, I finally surrendered to God's mission call and the call to singleness, and today I am writing the Scott story for all to read.

With the advent of social media, I became curious and was able to find Scott. He is married with children. He has a large home, and I truly hope he is happy. Truly … I mean it. Yes, I wonder why Scott stopped writing, but I doubt I will ever discover the answer to that question. However, I do know God stepped in because "His grace is sufficient for me." This is a lesson in spiritual warfare that I need to learn every day and one that God is still fighting on my behalf.

Questions for Individual or Group Study

1.   Without giving into the tendency to give a "Sunday School Answer," what is your human response to the idea – **We often have to recognize that the first battle in spiritual warfare is with the one that we fight with ourselves. The battle that we fight to release one's personal ambitions and dreams in order to achieve God's better plans for us. This is perhaps the hardest and longest-running battle of them all.**

2.   My daddy believed his scar (his cleft palate) was a limitation – something that held him back in his service to God. Is there something in your life that you believe holds you back? Is this your thorn or an excuse? If it is an excuse – what are you going to do to let it go?

3.   Do you have a "Scott Story?" What has/is God teaching you through your own story? Is the fact that you might never get the answer to your questions like I will probably never get the answer to mine alright with you or are you resisting the unknown?

3

Spiritual Warfare Is Often About a Service Concept
(Ephesians 6:10-13)

We must realize that spiritual warfare is an impossible fight without utilizing the gifts given to us by God and without the power of teamwork. However, we must also recognize that only God's gifts have the power, not our own ability to use them.

Suppose you were like me and grew up as a child of the 1970s, especially in Baptist churches in the South. In that case, you will recognize this song from Vacation Bible School or children's church, or any occasion that children were gathered together and the Christian workers were looking for something or anything to take up time:

I may never march in the infantry,
Ride in the cavalry,
Shoot the artillery,
I may never fly o'er the enemy.
But I'm in the Lord's Army! Yes, Sir![9]

It was a fun song for children to sing and expelled a lot of childhood energy, especially if you included all the hand motions. As to the question that some might raise about possibly glamorizing warfare for children, that is a discussion issue for another time and place.

The point of this chapter is that we are indeed in a spiritual battle and we are in the Lord's army but not in the way many expect or anticipate. And while many people go straight to verses 14-18 in Ephesians 6 to get armor ready for the battle, it would be foolhardy to go past verses 10-13 for it would leave us unprepared for the struggle we face daily as believers in Jesus. It would be like trying to march into a skirmish without the proper boots, shoot without cleaning one's gun, or attempting to fly without taking one flight lesson. You might start strong but I doubt you will finish – or you might finish but with a deafening thud.

---

[9] I was unable to find any authorial or historical information for the song. It is #517 in the *New National Baptist Hymnal* (21st Century Edition) but beyond that, it is anyone's guess as to the backstory to the writing of this children's song. For more information, go to **https://hymnary.org/hymn/NNBH2001/page/646n'ssong**. Accessed on 7 December 2024.

Ephesians 6:10-13 … More Than Just About Armor

I have to confess that I have never been the most athletic of individuals. The only sport I was ever good at was volleyball, which was only because I was left-handed and had a weird-looking serve. I could also aim my serve at the weakest player on the opposing team, and I could scout out who that player was during warm-ups. Therefore, and aside from volleyball, I was often one of the last players chosen for what I will describe as medieval-style games such as Dodge Ball or Red Rover. Can you tell I **hated** those sadistic, Machiavellian games?

I was never good at dodging the ball, and my large, nerdy head seemed an easy target for those athletic types – even if aiming for the head was supposed to be illegal. As far as it relates to Red Rover, I have skinny arms and I have never had a good grip. Therefore, I was an easy target for being run through by someone stronger than me, and I could never break through two arms when it was called out for "Red Rover, Red Rover, let Amy come over."

Interestingly enough, however, Red Rover has a great application to the idea of biblical spiritual warfare when one researches the history of this game. The origins of Red Rover date back to either the 1700s or 1800s, and more than likely to Great Britain (but possibly Germany). In the United Kingdom, the game was often called "British Bulldog" or "Bar the Door," and had its genesis as a war game for children. Essentially, the idea of the game in England was that the children played "Bar the Door" while their fathers were off fighting wars on the continent.[10] The idea was that they would be learning the importance of loyalty and togetherness and coming to terms with what their fathers, perhaps even their older brothers, might be experiencing on the battlefields and trenches of France or Germany.

However, we can also see that no individual can win Red Rover (i.e., the illustration of spiritual warfare for this chapter) on their own. It takes a team effort. Indeed, it takes the whole group to win many of the spiritual battles we face as we grow in our Christian walk. Therefore, we can never be Rambo or even the mighty Chuck Norris in this spiritual life. We must be a unit, a platoon, a battalion, or we will lose. Find me a spiritual hermit and you will find someone who is ineffective in their work for the kingdom of God.

And while we have often been taught in Sunday School classes or those small group Bible studies produced in Nashville that Ephesians 6:10-18 is a

---

[10] John Elmore, "The Timeless Tale of Red Rover: Unraveling the Mystery Behind the Classic Playground Game," available online at **https://thetechylife.com/whats-the-meaning-behind-red-rover/**; accessed 10 December 2024.

personal battle, it is not, regardless of who the author is.[11] Therefore, we need to see that this passage is about the community of faith – whether it be the community of the family, the community of women in the church, or the church community itself. This is why the armor does not fit well when we try to put it on alone. This is why the battles so often are lost when we fight them alone – because we are tilting at those very real windmills of spiritual issues as a lonely Don Quixote when we need a host of Sancho Panza's standing beside us.[12]

Be Strong in the Lord – v. 10

In the late 1980s and early 1990s, a group of strongmen on Christian television (TBN) traveled across the United States in school auditoriums and churches, led by John Jacobs. The group called "The Power Team" performed acts of physical strength like breaking handcuffs, tearing phonebooks in half (FYI – actual phonebooks are something that would have to be explained to the younger generation today), and performing karate chops on giant blocks of ice that crumbled as if they were nothing but shaved ice for snow cones. However, and like many of the Christian "sideshows" that rise and fall with time, this team of muscular men did fall within a few years. Financial irregularities and moral questions about their personal lives brought down Jacobs' version of "The Power Team," and today's 2.0 version is much smaller and less "powerful" than the original production.[13]

There is nothing wrong with Christian men and women having muscles and strong physiques, which is ironic for me to write, for I am typing this sentence with my skinny arms. Yet since my heart attack in November 2019, I have become much more aware of what goes into my body and how I need to take care of my outer shell as I serve the kingdom of God. But …

---

[11] Lifeway Press has recently produced a Bible study for women that follows this argument. This is not a correct understanding of the passage.

[12] Miquel de Cervantes Saavedra, *Don Quixote* (1605). Considered by some to be the first novel, *Don Quixote* is the story of an aging noble who longs for a return to the days of honor and Chivalry. Don Quixote would be considered in today's world as experiencing dementia, but his companion, Sancho Panza, while full of irony and sarcasm, is also loyal and protective of him.

[13] Rick Paulas, "The Power Team Was the Bloody, Evangelical Freakshow That Ruled the 80s," *Vice,* 4 February 2015, available online at **https://www.vice.com/en/article/evangelical-freak-show-the-power-team-were-christian-superstars-of-the-80s-456/**; accessed 18 December 2024. Please note that the article contains language that may not be suitable for Christian audiences, but it provides a fair representation of what happened to "The Power Team" in relation to their rise and fall.

"be(ing) strong in the Lord," and in the power of His might" has nothing to do with the outer shell of our being.

In fact, I would argue that the translation "be strong" is not the ideal way of expressing the concept of what Paul was seeking to convey to the church at Ephesus. The word in Greek (ἐνδυναμοῦσθε) is better understood as "to be empowered" or in essence that we need to be **made strong** "in [or by] the Lord" because we cannot be strong in and of ourselves. Additionally, and I would argue that this is most important for understanding this section, this verb is not in the first person but in the second person plural. But why is this so important? Paul was telling the church and also us today that we cannot be strong by ourselves.

Yes ... we can only be strong as a united group – as a whole, as an *Ekklesia* (community) – and believing that we can be empowered by ourselves is nothing but a falsehood that will make us weak in the end. The verb is also an imperative (a command) as are all the verbs in Ephesians 6:10-13. These verbs are a command for we must recognize that it is in the Lord's strength alone that we can even hope to approach any level of God's strength and not our false weakness against the spiritual battles we are called to face. God's might is absolute and our power is less than even verifiable.

The Importance of "So That" (v. 11-13)

As I wrote in chapter one, I believe that our Christian culture has taken the phrase "spiritual warfare" and made it all about demon slaying instead of discipleship training. Now, you might look ahead to verses 12-13 and believe my thesis has been debunked. The next verses are filled with images of our Christian nightmares – principalities, powers, darkness, and wickedness. However, I would argue that these verses, along with verses 14-18, actually support my argument, and it all begins with the phrase – "so that."

"So that" or "that" in the KJV explains to us why we are commanded to "Put on the full armor of God." We need this full armor **so that** we can stand/continue/hold/be steadfast against the schemes of the devil." We cannot fight what we are called to fight again – whether it be earthly or spiritual – unless we are fully trained and/or discipled to do it. However, and far too often, believers want to jump into warfare, without going through basic training, and they want to go into warfare fighting those spiritual forces in those heavenly places alone. Forgetting that there are battles to fight here in the grit and grime here on earth.

When this happens ... the believer is unprepared, and destined for defeat after defeat after defeat, and often looks around, blaming everyone else for the defeat except himself. John Bunyan in *Pilgrim's Progress* and C. S. Lewis in *Pilgrim's Regress* both warned of such adventures, yet we still find ourselves trying to fight alone and without discipleship spiritual warfare training, and yet still wonder why we end up with battle scars and defeats.

Yes, there are real spiritual issues out there, both in the heavenly realms and in the faces of those in the McDonald's booth across from you. However, each case does not require holy water and a gigantic cross to hide behind each time. The people with satanic tattoos on their faces sitting beside you on the plane need the Gospel. The homeless man who is schizophrenic with voices in his head needs the Gospel. The woman who attempts to stop Christian prayer groups at the local schools because she is an atheist needs the Gospel. Are we prepared and discipled as Christians, churches, small groups, and families to reach out to them with the Gospel and not modern versions of the Satanic Panic that gripped the United States in the 1990s?

Each one of these examples are vivid truths of verse twelve. It is our response that illustrates or reveals our spiritual warfare preparation. Do we attempt to trade seats on the plane or do we engage in conversation with the tattooed people and try to find out what motivated them to put those symbols on their bodies? Do we attempt "to cast out those demons" for our glory or do we seek to find help for the homeless man that will heal the mind, body, and soul? Do we create a firestorm in the community that divides everyone over the issue of prayer or do we pray for the woman and seek to meet with her privately to find out why she is so opposed to prayer groups? Ultimately, do we find ways to bring the Gospel into the conversation or ourselves into the limelight?

Yes, as verse thirteen tells us, there is spiritual wickedness in the heavenly places. I have seen it. I have looked into the eyes of a young woman who had "dabbled" in Wiccan and been changed by her walk on the dark side. I have also been able to share the Gospel with her because I earned her trust because she saw me studying my Bible and praying consistently. I have walked into an event promoting Kabbalah (Jewish mysticism) and been able to share the Gospel with over 200 people, even though I planned to observe and learn about this mysticism as it is attracting so many Jewish people. The reason was that I had several Christians praying for me the entire time I was there. I was not alone in the fight, and that is the point of Ephesians 6:10-13. We cannot fight our spiritual battles or grow in the faith alone.

There was a terrible movie in the late 1990s that became a disturbing, but sadly impactful TV series for young people called *Buffy the Vampire Slayer*. The show's premise is that a young teenage girl was destined to be a vampire slayer – told you it was a disturbing television show. Every episode began with this phrase penned by its creator, Joss Whedon – *"In every generation, there is a chosen one. She alone will stand against the vampires, the demons, and the forces of darkness.*

She is the slayer." Somehow, I believe Whedon did not realize Jesus already won the battle against the demons and forces of darkness … on the cross!

Joss Whedon's terrible movie and disturbing TV series were at the forefront of the vampire phenomenon that captivated millions of young girls and culminated with the *Twilight* series. Whedon introduced untold millions to a dark side of life that needs to be counteracted, and it has now been discovered that the creator of this series has his own dark side.[14]

While we rightly can criticize Whedon and his Buffy character, Christians for some reason love to dabble in darkness for some bizarre reason. We seem to be more inclined to find the demon under every rock, rather than devoting ourselves to discipleship and putting on the armor of God to fight for the future of the Christian faith. Yes, some events happen that can only be explained as the "spiritual forces of wickedness in the heavenly places;" but, the rulers, the powers, and the dark forces on this planet need to be confronted as they are very real as well. These forces do not require exorcisms, but rather spiritual exercises, such as Bible study, prayer, and personal discipline, which are described in more detail in verses 14-18. Yes, I know these exercises are not nearly as "much fun" as demon slaying, but a great deal more edifying and equipping to the kingdom of God. God does not need a Rambo, Chuck Norris, or even a vampire slayer named Buffy. He desires more soldiers in the Lord's Army. Yes, sir!

Questions for Individual or Group Study

1.   Without giving into the tendency to give a "Sunday School Answer," what is your human response to the idea – **We must realize that spiritual warfare is an impossible fight without utilizing the gifts given to us by God and without the power of teamwork. However, we must also recognize that only God's gifts have the power, not our own ability to use them.**

2.   How often do you try to fight the spiritual battles alone? How frequently are you successful in these fights? What is it about American Christians that we believe we can Rambo our way through the Christian struggles alone?

3.   Do you ever feel as if you are fighting your spiritual battles in a *Don Quixote* fashion – fighting them in a windmill fashion? Do you need one, two,

---

[14] "Joss Whedon: Buffy and Justice League Director Denies Misconduct Claims," BBC (18 January 2022), available online at **https://www.bbc.com/news/entertainment-arts-60036933**; accessed 19 December 2024. Whedon also portrays himself as an atheist -- **https://www.celebatheists.com/wiki/Joss_Whedon**.

or a dozen Sancho Panza's in your life to help you in your spiritual battles? What keeps you from finding your allies for the battles? Are you a spiritual hermit?

4.   Why are so many Christians seemingly more drawn to the dark side than to spiritual exercises like prayer, Bible study, and spiritual discipline? What is it about "fighting demons" that attracts so many people?

5.   Do you agree with the author that discipleship has fallen on "hard times" in churches? If so, why? If not, why not?

4

Spiritual Warfare Is Often About Finishing
Even When We Want to Stop and Quit
(2 Timothy 4:1-5)

We need to recognize that spiritual warfare is about finishing even when we want to fall apart mentally, spiritually, and physically. Sometimes winning the spiritual battle in the Christian life is just about finishing the spiritual fight.

If you read the dedication to this book, you can probably guess I was a daddy's girl. As a Southerner now living in New York State, I have the unique privilege of always being a daddy's girl regardless of how old I live to be. This is one of the benefits of speaking with somewhat of a Southern drawl – we are allowed to use the term "daddy" concerning our father regardless of how old we are or how long our daddy has been gone from this earth.

My sweet and truly humble daddy died when I was thirty years old at the age of 66 from an abdominal aneurysm after he had devoted almost 30 years to full-time Christian service. In many ways, he passed away as a broken man, both physically and emotionally, after one of his final churches broke his heart over their lack of commitment to God's commandments and their willingness to overlook sin in the camp (i.e., think of the story of Achan from the book of Joshua). His final sermon on 2 July 2000 was from Jeremiah about the potter and the clay and being willing to be broken repeatedly so that we can be molded into the image that best reflects what the Great Designer wants for our lives. And while I have heard this sermon of my dad's more than once, I cannot make myself listen to the tape given to me by the church and hear my dad's final sermon and his voice for I know my heart could not take it.

Daddy's biblical heroes were Enoch and Noah. Two men from the Hebrew Scriptures who might not be considered "hero timber" by some, but they were for Jack Downey. Noah was faithful, and even though he had only seven others to join him on the Ark, the Ark builder persevered in obedience. Enoch, as well, was faithful – faithful enough to be found worthy not to face death and walked "home" with God one night instead of heading back to his earthly dwelling.

Those two words – faithful and obedient – were important to my dad. Especially when the times were dark and the situation was dreary and in many ways, Jack Downey went home to Heaven on 4 July 2000 when he reached the bedroom, despite hurting from a stomach pain that he did not realize was the last discomfort of his life, to reach the arms of the woman he had loved for almost forty years for a final embrace. For my dad had been obedient to God

25

when it would have been much "easier" to compromise to earthly suggestions to look the other way at sinful situations.

We could say the same thing about the man born as Saul of Tarsus. According to Christian tradition, the Apostle Paul ended his life at the Mamertine Prison – in many ways forgotten and alone, except for Luke and a few others, based on the words of 2 Timothy 4.[15] He had been abandoned by Demas (v. 10), and Alexander the Coppersmith (v. 14) had done him evil. Verse sixteen are the words of a man at the end of his life who would have disagreed with John Donne's words from *Meditation XVII* – "No man is an island, Entire of itself; Every man is a piece of the continent, A part of the main."[16] For in the Mamertine Prison, and shortly before his martyrdom, Paul appeared in many ways to believe himself to be utterly alone, yet we can still find in his words to Timothy a man to be faithful and obedient – even if broken and despondent.

This is an important lesson that we can learn today. Spiritual warfare is not glamorous. Spiritual warfare is not always victorious. Spiritual warfare is often bloody and filled with heartache and death. Yet … it is a warfare, a battle, that must be fought to the end. It is a battle that must be fought when we want to hide under the bedcovers. It is a battle that must be fought when we want to run away and hide. It is a battle that must be fought when the only thing we want to do is surrender. For perhaps the two most important words of our Christian walk should be faithfulness and obedience.

Before we begin to consider Paul's final words before his deliverance to the streets of gold, I would like to stop a moment and consider his final message to the Ephesian church in Acts 20:24. These words he shared with the people of Ephesus before he headed to Jerusalem and began his final years of chains and imprisonment, are my life verse – *"But none of these things move me, neither count I my life dear unto myself, so that I might finish my course with joy, and the ministry, which I have received of the Lord Jesus, to testify the gospel of the grace of God."* I

---

[15] Derrick G. Jeter, "Historical Background of Paul's Final Imprisonment," Insight for Living (4 August 2017), available online at **https://www.insight.org/resources/article-library/individual/historical-background-of-paul-s-final-imprisonment**; accessed 23 December 2024.

[16] John Donne, The Works of John Donne, vol. 3, *Devotions Upon Emergent Occasions*, "Meditation XVII," Henry Alford, ed. (London: John Alford, 1839): 574-75, available online at **https://luminarium.org/sevenlit/donne/meditation17.php**; accessed 23 December 2024.

believe they also testify to the life of missionary William Whiting Borden (1887-1913).[17]

Borden technically never made it to his final mission designation of inland China, as he died after contracting spinal meningitis in Egypt and died from the illness in less than three weeks. Still, his influence – including bequeathing the bulk of his estate as the son of a silver magnate to Hudson Taylor's China Inland Mission – and his heart for the lost of the world should not be forgotten. Borden influenced countless Christians in the early part of the twentieth century to dedicate themselves to the mission field much like the martyrdom of the Auca 5 (Jim Elliot, Nate Saint, Pete Fleming, Roger Youderian, and Ed McCully) did in the mid-20th century. And the tragic fact that many today will not know who Borden or the Auca 5 were is a tragedy for our churches. Their faithfulness and obedience, including Rachel Saint (sister of Nate Saint) and the widows – including Elisabeth Elliot and Olive Fleming – should always be remembered. The legacy they leave behind illustrates Paul's words in 2 Timothy 4, as well as the possible legendary testimony of William Borden's "No Reserves, No Retreats, No Regrets."

By necessity, I must use the term "legendary testimony" because the Bible in which Borden possibly wrote these phrases has never been found.[18] So did he write these phrases in his Bible to indicate his willingness to go to an area of China to witness to 15 million Chinese Muslims who had never heard the Gospel in the early years of the twentieth century? We will never know for certain, even though one of his biographers does mention the Bible and the statements. Truly … it does not matter in the grand scope of eternity because William Borden lived the truth of these statements every day of his short life. I also know that in one of my older Bibles, these phrases are written in the margins of Acts 20:24.

Paul's Charge to Timothy (and to Us) – 4:1-5

While on a personal retreat, I once wrote in a prayer journal the following words as it relate to verse one:

---

[17] The short life of missionary William Borden is a fascinating tale of faithfulness and obedience. A full account of his life can be found at Jayson Casper, "The Forgotten Final Resting Place of William Borden," *Christianity Today* (24 February 2017), available online at **https://www.christianitytoday.com/2017/02/forgotten-final-resting-place-of-william-borden/**; accessed 29 December 2024.

[18] Ibid.

"Commissioned before the ever-examining face of God to go and do…"

Being charged, being commissioned, and being called by the King of the Universe is something that clenches my stomach. It humbles me beyond any explanation. Yet, it is something that I must do because I have been commanded to do so for the Messiah Jesus, who died for my salvation, the Jesus who rose again for me so that I can have hope in his resurrection, as 1 Corinthians 15 reminds us. And while I am not a pastor as Timothy was to the church at Ephesus, I am a missionary and a teacher. Those who are reading these words also have gifts and a calling given to them by God and should not have to apologize for them either.

It should be noted that I am one who does not believe in women pastors or deacons (and perhaps that is a reason to write another book), but I do understand my place, my role, and my calling from God, who alone can and has and does call me for his kingdom purposes. This is also the message that I would love to share with the readers as well. We must stop questioning ourselves because of what others say or write or seek to impose upon us. If you are a Christian woman, you have a kingdom purpose. If you are a divorced man with a tragic past, you have a kingdom purpose. If you are a young person, you have a wide-open kingdom purpose that is often only limited by your self-defeating limitations.

Why can I say this with such confidence? The five verbs that Paul communicated to a very young Timothy in verse two – preach, be ready (be instant), reprove, rebuke, and exhort – are all in the imperative/command tense. Now I know that some will see the word "preach" and automatically see this word as only belonging to the pastoral role. However, and I am going to mention my daddy again, he always taught there was a difference between a pastor and a preacher. His exact words were – "Men are called to be pastors; **everyone** is called to be a preacher. We are all given the Great Commission. Get out there and share."

Without going into the Greek until everyone has their eyes roll back in their heads, the word for preach(er) in the New Testament is *kerusso* which means to herald or proclaim or publish specifically the Gospel. The word for pastor can be understood by one of three words – *presbuteros* (elder), *poimen* (pastor), *episkopos* (bishop/overseer). Aside from gaining insight into how two mainline denominations developed their names, the terms themselves also provide insight into the responsibility of the pastoral role – guidance, shepherding, oversight,[19] as well as preaching the Gospel. So, while few are called to the pastorate, everyone is called to proclaim/preach the Gospel to the world.

Paul wrote to Timothy, the pastor of Ephesus, in verses 3-5, and to us today, why those five imperative verbs were so essential. There is a time coming when people will not endure sound doctrine (i.e., put up with) but will instead seek views, beliefs, and values that make themselves "feel better" about their choices in life. Incidentally, Paul was not writing about those who live outside of the church world … he was writing to Timothy about those sitting before him in the Ephesus church. These are the "church hoppers" who jump from one church to another, trying to find the pastor who will scratch their itch and not step on their toes. These are the people who will leave one house of worship for another because they have a worship team that is livelier or a youth group with more teenagers in it, even if the depth of teaching offered is less than nil. The Bible scholar Gordon Fee would probably liken these churchgoers to dabblers or amateurs in the faith who are only looking for the next theological flavor of the month to follow.[20]

It did not improve for Timothy after the martyrdom of Paul, and it is not any better for us today.[21] This is why Paul appears to be compelled to command (imperative tense again) in verse five to do four things after he is gone from this world. The **first command** is to watch [himself] or be self-controlled in all things … and this is often harder than you might imagine.

As a single missionary and the president of Tzedakah Ministries, I feel as if I have to be more diligent about my actions and thoughts and deeds than many men. I am being watched for the slightest misstep and failure. The moral decisions I make in my personal life revolve around the idea that I must not fail in my missionary calling.

For example, when I moved to New York for the first time in 2000, I had an apartment in Queens. My landlord was an older Catholic man who knew I was Baptist but thought I must be some sort of "Baptist Nun" because I

---

[19] Ralph F. Wilson, "Elders, Pastors, and Overseers: A Word Study," Joyful Heart Renewal Ministries, available online at **https://www.joyfulheart.com/scholar/elders.htm**; accessed 31 December 2024. The terminology is one of the reasons I hold to a male-only place for pastors but there are other reasons as well.

[20] Gordon D. Fee, *1 and 2 Timothy, Titus*, New International Biblical Commentary (vol. 13), NT ed., W. Ward Gasque (Peabody, MA: Hendrickson Publishers, 1984), 286.

[21] Ibid.

never had male guests and my female guests only stayed for a short time and never overnight, except when my mama came to visit from Texas. His son Vincent was a priest, and he shared this "Baptist Nun" story with me when I moved out because his father so respected my personal lifestyle.

The **second and third commands** of endurance and doing the work of an evangelist can be tied together because evangelism is often tied together with the idea of hardship. A person will and/or can experience suffering for sharing the Gospel. It may be overt, as in Paul's martyrdom. It can be covert, such as not getting the raise or promotion a person might have wanted. It could also be watching someone that we love rejecting the truth of Jesus and entering into eternity without Jesus. This grief that we personally endure is greater than we ever dreamed possible. And I truly believe that of all three sufferings, knowing that a friend or a family member rejects the Gospel is a greater suffering than even personal martyrdom. Paul's lament in Romans 9:3 expresses this pain even more eloquently than I can put into words. However, and even now, I am visualizing precious friends who will not join me in Heaven one day, and my soul is ravished by their eternal separation from Jesus.

The **final command** in verse five is written in the KJV as "make full proof" and in other translations as "fulfill." It can also be expressed as 'finish your ministry.' This is the essence of the focus of this chapter on spiritual warfare. There are too many individuals, whether they be pastors, missionaries, or others in Christian service (including laypeople), who do not complete their work because they give up, lose their will to fight, or are defeated in their personal lives by one issue or another. We must complete our ministry, for to fail to do so is to fail the one who gave us our calling.

Paul, in the remainder of 2 Timothy 4, writes of those who failed to finish, such as Demas and Alexander the Coppersmith. He writes of unnamed individuals who did not stand with him when he was brought to prison for the final time. He writes of individuals who stood with him faithfully – Priscilla, Aquilla, Luke, Mark, and Titus. Ultimately, Paul writes that he is ready to go home to Heaven because he has finished the course and kept the faith. This is what we must do as well, because sometimes finishing is the greatest spiritual battle of them all.

The giant of the First Great Awakening, Jonathan Edwards, who preached the sermon that we still consider one of the greatest evangelistic sermons of American history – "Sinners in the Hands of an Angry God" experienced one of the greatest letdowns in pastoral history. Less than a decade after delivering the sermon, he was actually fired from his church in 1750 in

Northampton, Massachusetts, over theological disputes within the church.[22] He lost his favorite daughter, Jerusha, and his protégé, David Brainerd, who was known for his missionary outreach to the indigenous Indian tribes of New England, died shortly before his dismissal. His grandson became the infamous and treasonous Aaron Burr, who murdered Alexander Hamilton in a duel in the early 1800s.

Indeed, Jonathan Edwards lost a great deal in the final years of his life. However, Edwards did not stop but finished well. Before dying in 1758 as the president of Princeton College, he followed in the footsteps of David Brainerd and became a missionary to the Native Americans, rather than taking over a cushy pastorate.[23] Simply speaking, Jonathan Edwards did not stop serving God but found another way of living out his testimony, finishing the work set before him. Yes, Edwards was not a perfect man as he did have two African slaves in his household, and that should be acknowledged, but he did fight the good fight and finished the course that was laid before him.

This is my encouragement to you if I can offer one. We must follow the example of Paul, Timothy, Jonathan Edwards (minus the horrific slavery aspect), my daddy, and others as well. For finishing the battle is sometimes the greatest spiritual battle that we will ever fight.

Questions for Individual or Group Study

1. Without giving into the tendency to give a "Sunday School Answer," what is your human response to the idea – **We need to recognize that spiritual warfare is about finishing even when we want to fall apart mentally, spiritually, and physically. Sometimes winning the spiritual battle in the Christian life is just about finishing the spiritual fight.**

2. Paul was very transparent about his feelings of discouragement in 2 Timothy 4 – the people who disappointed him and the people who abandoned him. Have you ever considered this aspect of 2 Timothy 4, or have you only considered Paul a "Super Christian" who never struggled? How does this perspective impact on your view of Paul, either in a positive or negative light? Does it make him more approachable? Or are you disappointed in Paul, who struggled with discouragement in the final years of his life?

3. Is there anything in the life of William Borden that can be of encouragement to you? His willingness to abandon wealth for the sake of the mission call is something that many find difficult to fathom today. Is there

---

[22] George M. Marsden, *Jonathan Edwards: A Life* (New Haven, CT: Yale University Press, 2003), 291-361.

[23] Ibid., 395-413.

something in your life that you would struggle to abandon for the "sake of the call"? What would it take for you to "give it up for Jesus"?

4.   Have you ever felt limited by another person when you sought to live out your calling for God's kingdom? Have you ever limited yourself? Why did it happen? Why did you allow it to happen? How do you respond to Paul's five imperative/command verbs in light of the calling that God has given you? Are you going to do something now or are you still going to be limited by circumstances?

5.   Which of the four commands in 2 Timothy 4:5 is the most difficult for you? Why? What do you have to do in order to gain victory over this command of Paul and of God?

6.   Did the end of Jonathan Edwards' life surprise you? Would you have been tempted to give up if you had experienced all that Edwards had experienced? Do not give the church answer to the previous question – be honest.

5

Spiritual Warfare Is Often a Human Battle
as Much as It Is a Spiritual Battle
(2 Corinthians 10:3-6)

We need to recognize that in spiritual warfare, the battle isn't about our natural abilities but whether we are willing to surrender our fears, doubts, and terrors to what sometimes feels like the unknown.

My first-grade teacher, Mrs. Virginia Dailey, is a Facebook friend today. I believe she looks the same, except for some gray hair, as first grade for me was almost fifty years ago. I am grateful that I do not look the same, as I was a scrawny thing back in 1976 with hair that couldn't decide whether it wanted to be red or brown. I also had the beginning of an awkward smile because of teeth that were not coming in right, and braces would arrive in high school after an appliance or two. Yes, I was the "Queen of the Nerds" in high school.

However, Mrs. Dailey was exceptionally kind to this precocious child who was the last child to be picked up on the first day of school because daddy read the handout wrong and thought I would be dismissed at the same time as my sixth-grade sister (two hours later). She waited with me and even bought me a Big Red to drink! Daddy rushed into the classroom about 45 minutes late, and I smiled at him with my red-lipped smile tinged by a soft drink. Mrs. Dailey assured him I was perfectly alright because she was getting to know her new student better.

Little could Mrs. Dailey imagine that this first day of school would turn into a year unlike any other for her. I soon taxed Mrs. Dailey's imagination as I finished all the assignments twice as fast as any other student. I read on a 3rd or 4th grade level when other students struggled to learn phonics. Truth be told, Mrs. Dailey (and she will always be Mrs. Dailey to me) was running out of assignments to give me, and soon she called for a teacher-parent meeting with Jack and Barbara Downey.

At this parent-teacher conference, Mrs. Dailey suggested to my parents that I remain in her classroom for the remainder of the year but advance to the second grade and begin third grade starting with the next school year. There was even consideration given to having me move to the fourth grade. My parents prayed about the decision and agreed to allow me to "skip" ahead one year, but thought it would be too hard for me to go ahead two years. They were right, as I was a late bloomer physically during my junior high years … another sad symptom of nerdiness.

When I received my PhD in Theology & Apologetics from Liberty University in 2016, I made a point to thank three teachers in the preface to my dissertation for their profound influence on my life. Mrs. Dailey was one of those three teachers, along with my sixth-grade reading teacher and my freshman college history professor. Three educators who encouraged me, believed in me, and never sought to hold me back from achieving my life goals.

Yet … being one of the smart kids does not always guarantee success in life. Yes, I was smart (i.e., Queen of the Nerds). Learning is one of my life passions, but acquiring knowledge is not always a ticket to success in this world. Serving God is not a *Jeopardy* contest, wherein knowing the answers to all the Bible trivia questions or living your life correctly ensures you will go home with the most honors. If anything, and in the world today, it almost guarantees that you will not.

This was the message that Paul sought to share with a church (Corinth) that almost continuously doubted his credentials of being an apostle – even though he was undoubtedly the smartest one of them all (Phil. 3:4-6). Paul did not have to prove it to them because his documents were already stamped as approved by God. Yet, it was an exercise he was called on to do in many places and for many people. It surely must have been a tiresome exercise that had to have weighed on Paul. However, it must have been something that he had to remind himself that this, too, was beyond his control. And … that is the point of this chapter on spiritual warfare – are we willing to surrender what we can control (intelligence, natural abilities) for only what God can control? Are we willing to let go and let God be God?

We Are Humans … But We Do Not Have to Act Like Humans (v. 3)

I have a confession to make. I am much more like the Apostle Paul than I would like to be. If you read his letters (epistles) closely, you get the sense that Paul knew he rubbed people the wrong way, and I know I can as well. Paul was respected because of his service to Jesus Messiah and his willingness to lay it "all on the altar," as the old hymn used to remind us.[24] Yet … Paul was never one to "win friends and influence people," as Dale Carnegie used to encourage people in his books and seminars. He fought with Peter and other church leaders. He was a fighter for a good cause, and I tend to be a righteous indignation fighter more than is often needed or even might be deemed necessary.

---

[24] E. A. Hoffman, "Is Your All on the Altar?," Hymnary.org, available online at **https://hymnary.org/text/you_have_longed_for_sweet_peace**; accessed 8 January 2025. It should be noted that Hoffman wrote the more well-known hymn "Leaning on the Everlasting Arms."

I always wanted to be more like the Apostle John. You know the disciple described in the Bible as "the disciple whom Jesus loved." The one who was able to see Jesus in his transcendent glory and was granted the honor of writing the book of Revelation. The one who lived long enough to take the Gospel personally to the second generation of the Christian church. The one whom everyone appears to like, love, and appreciate, even when his letters (1, 2, and 3 John) had some tough messages for the churches. No one ever questioned John's credentials like they questioned Paul's authenticity, and I can empathize with what appears to me, at least, to be some consternation in this passage. Yet, Paul writes in verse three what is, in essence, an acknowledgment that while he is human, he will not respond as a human.

This simple verse, "For though we walk in the flesh, we do not war after [according to] the flesh," is a tough one for me. It is the essence of seeing that, as humans, we do not have to behave like humans. It is also very reminiscent of Jesus' final prayer for the disciples before he was arrested at Gethsemane (John 17:14, 16). And it all boils down to the old adage – "Be in the world but not of the world." And it is very, very hard to live out that saying when the people hurling the most hurtful insults are sometimes doing so from the pews and/or chairs in the Sunday School classes.

We have to remember that our flesh (our humanity) will be lost in this war fought in the spiritual realm. In my flesh, I struggle with fear, doubt, and occasional bouts of terror when I should live in trust, faith, and belief. Humanly – I struggle with trusting people to live up to their promises because I have been disappointed in the past. Humanly – I struggle with why **it seems** (and that is an important phrase) that I am always there with a life preserver available for others, but those same people often will let me drown.

Instead, I must focus on the only outstretched hand that matters and trust in Him alone. This is a spiritual reality and a manifestation of spiritual warfare. And … that was what Paul meant when he wrote in verse three that he would not engage or wage war (***strateuo***), which can also be defined as the "warring lusts against the soul."[25] Our humanity, our warring lusts, which is

---

[25] The website BibleHub.com provides an excellent Greek lexicon for anyone but especially for the individual who wants to begin a study of the original languages. There was a statement there underneath the information for the ***Strong's Lexicon*** that is especially helpful for understanding this passage – "In the New Testament, it (war[fare]) is often used metaphorically to describe the spiritual warfare that believers engage in against sin, the flesh, and spiritual forces of evil. It conveys the idea of active participation in a struggle or conflict, emphasizing the disciplined and committed nature of the Christian life." For additional information go to **Strong's Greek: 4754. στρατεύομαι (strateuó) -- To wage war, to serve as a soldier, to engage in spiritual warfare**; accessed 15 January 2024.

such an apt description of our flesh, can be crushed when people disappoint, but as Paul illustrates, there is so much more to fight for in this world. In fact, the apostle begins to point out this truth in verse four.

Weapons of Our Warfare (v. 4-6)

My dad kept it a secret from us (my sister and me) all of his life, and we only discovered it after he died. We knew that mama saw daddy as her knight in shining armor, but we never understood why until after his death, when the secrets of mama's childhood began to tumble out. It was then that we began to realize that our grandmother had emotionally and verbally abused my mother for most of her childhood.

We all knew that mama's mother (this is how I today refer to the woman as my sister tells me it is inappropriate to refer to her by her first name) was a difficult woman. She was an angry person who belittled my sweet grandpa for as long as I could remember. There was no kinder or more Christian man than Clarence Butler, and everyone in our family – aunts, uncles, cousins, and so on – wondered how this wonderful individual could stay with a woman as angry as she was. Yet … Clarence Butler genuinely loved her and stood by her side throughout the years of their marriage.

However, it was not until daddy died that the secrets of the abuse came out. Daddy was my mom's protector and guard against mama's mother and with daddy gone, what was once secret began to become known. One of the most vindictive tactics of mama's mother was to be silent for hours or even days towards her daughter. This tactic was not about punishment but just to be silent for silence's sake.

My mama died in 2020 at the age of 78, and even with the passing of almost sixty years since she had left her parents' home, silence was the greatest fear of my mother's life. Silence, being alone, could reduce this amazing woman who loved everyone and gave so much to anyone in need to a child-like state. In truth, having to leave her in the hospital in the worst days of COVID and knowing I could not be with her broke me because I knew it would break her … and it did. Incidentally, this was why I brought her home for the final week of her life, because I wanted her to hold the hands of those who loved her most, as she could not die alone in a hospital, as so many others were. I could not allow it.

Anyway, I share this personal story with you because mama could well identify with verses 4-6 of this passage given what she experienced as a child. Why do I know this to be true? She forgave her mother – an issue that I am still working on in my life because the woman hurt my mama. She was able to pull down the stronghold of abuse and not repeat the cycle of abuse with her daughters. No, mama was not perfect, but we were told that we were loved and shown love every day of our lives. Silence was not allowed in our home when I was growing up. It was never messy, but it was filled with laughter, love, and lots and lots of sound.

Mama was able to accomplish this feat because she had my daddy on her side, and she leaned upon God constantly. She fell at times, and hints of her mother would escape, but when she saw those glimpses, she would crumble in shame for that moment and resolve to be better than she had been before. This is why Paul wrote the phrase of casting down (or overthrowing) the arguments/imaginations in the present participle – for it is not something we can only do once.

For fighting whatever battle we must face is an ongoing battle that must be fought and defeated over and over again. Doing so will result in those thoughts being brought into captivity to obedience to Christ (v. 5b-6). And, yes, obedience is not always fun or easy, but it is the final result of the fight – the spiritual warfare that will always be ongoing in our lives.

I struggle with silence as well, but it is not the same kind of silence that mama experienced from her mother. I struggle with spiritual silence at times. Sometimes I feel as if God is silent towards me, and that terrifies me. The questions I ask – What have I done, God? Are you mad at me, God? – race across my mind in what seems to be a mile-a-minute. They are followed up by other questions – Why couldn't I be loved by people like other people are? Why must I always feel beleaguered?

I have come to realize that silence from God is different than the abuse that my mama experienced from her mother. Sometimes it is not silence, but the quiet voice of God, because I am not listening to His still, small voice (1 Kings 19:11-13). Sometimes it is because I have become distracted by my own voice that is trying to drown out the voice of God. Sometimes, it is because God is silent, not because He is punishing me, but because I need to be drawn back closer to Him, and silence is the only option to get my attention.

I have learned that my thoughts must be focused on God's purpose, not on what I think should be, not on what I believe ought to be, and most definitely not on what I believe is fair. I have learned that my reasoning is not always God's reality, and that is a hard lesson to learn. I have also learned one of the hardest lessons of all – that my mind can be right from a worldly perspective but wrong from a heavenly perspective.

This is the process (and I am still on it) to finding the ultimate end of verse 6 – having a fulfilled or completed obedience. Spiritual warfare is continual and requires a focus that is hard and, at times, impossible to achieve. Many in this world will say that spiritual warfare is not fair, but it is ultimately good and right by God's design if we desire to walk and war with God.

This is what Paul understood in 2 Corinthians 10:3-6 and what we need to honor today as well. By doing so, we will be able to fight the good fight, as 2 Timothy mentions, walk with Jesus in the Garden, as will be discussed in the next chapter, and understand the messages of Jeremiah, as will be discussed in greater detail in future chapters of this work.

Questions for Individual or Group Study

1.   Without giving into the tendency to give a "Sunday School Answer," what is your human response to the idea – **We need to recognize that in spiritual warfare, the battle isn't about our natural abilities but whether we are willing to surrender our fears, doubts, and terrors to what sometimes feels like the unknown.**

2.   Have you ever seen yourself – either positively or negatively – in one of the individuals in the Bible? How did that impact your perspective of yourself and/or of that Biblical character? Have you ever considered that this individual might just be present in the Scripture, warts and all, to allow us today to recognize that God can use us just as he used Paul, John, or even Rahab the Harlot?

3.   What is the stronghold in your life that needs to be confronted and overcome? What is holding you back from confronting the issue? Or … have you already faced it? If so, what lessons about yourself and God did you learn in the battle?

4.   Have you ever struggled with the silence of God? What was your response to it or God? Mother Teresa struggled with God's silence most of her ministry life. She wrote in a letter the following – *"As for me, the silence and the emptiness is so great, that I look and do not see, — Listen and do not hear — the tongue moves but does not speak … I want you to pray for me — that I let Him have free hand."* What is your response to Mother Teresa's attitude to the silence of God?

6

Spiritual Warfare Is About a Recognition That to Finish … We Often Have to Go Through Dark Nights
(Jesus at Gethsemane Passages)

We need to realize that as believers in Jesus, there is no escaping the truth and the reality that there are real emotional components to spiritual warfare. Even though we might and sometimes are not able to see the end of spiritual warfare while we are going through it, we often still have to go "through the dark night of our soul" to reach the end of it. There is value in these experiences even when we are desperate to escape them.

Twice I have been to the Garden of Gethsemane and both times I wept like a child who lost their favorite blanket. The first time I was with a tour group of other Christians, my friend Sheila G. led the tour along with my pastor, Bruce Zimmerman. Sheila had connections and knew someone who could get our group into the section with the oldest trees in the garden. Some of the trees were hundreds of years old, and I like to imagine that some of those trees could have been seedlings at the time when Jesus walked into the Garden the night before he was crucified.

I searched for the oldest tree I could find and spent several minutes praying for the salvation of the Jewish people, as well as praying that I would become a better missionary to them. Unbeknownst to me, one of my fellow tour group members took a picture of me while I was praying and sent me a copy because my posture and face in prayer so moved her. I still have the image in a frame to remind me of the emotions I felt at that moment under the olive trees in Gethsemane.

The second time I visited Gethsemane, I was with my sweet mama. This was her first and only trip to Israel and she was absorbing every moment – especially since daddy had never been able to make the trip. While at Gethsemane, we quickly went through the Church of All Nations (aka Basilica of the Agony) because neither one of us were great fans of churches built on top of historical and/or religious landmarks. I showed mama the old trees that were protected from tourists unless you knew someone like Sheila G. and then I stopped for a moment on the steps of the church. It was at that moment of stopping on the church steps that I began to weep like I had never wept before or since in Israel – and I have been there four separate times.

I cried on those steps because I looked up and saw the Mount of Olives. I sobbed because I looked down and saw what is called the Via Dolorosa, or the path to Golgotha and the tomb. It suddenly struck me that on the night before Jesus was crucified, he also stood in this garden and could look down to see the true agony that awaited him "tomorrow" at the cross, and then look up to see the victory that awaited him at the second coming. It hit me all at once that the Garden was the place, the site, and the point of no return for Jesus.

Those words – "Not as I will, but as you will" – are still some of the most remarkable words ever spoken in the history of humanity. The final temptation, the final test, and the final battle were in a garden in which Jesus could see "Friday's pain" and the second coming at the same time. I could not help but weep, and all mama could do was hold me as I sought to explain to her the reason for my tears through words garbled by sobs.

Jesus' tears on that fateful night before the crucifixion were for us today as much as it was for anyone. This is why I wrote in the theme for the chapter the following words – **"For even though we might and sometimes not be able to see the end of spiritual warfare even while we are going through it, we often still have to go "through the dark night of our soul," to reach the end of it."**[26] For the battle experiences of the dark night are painful and often long, but they are for our purification and to prepare us for what lies ahead. And, yes, I once told mama that I often wondered if the light at the end of the tunnel was actually nothing more than just a train barreling towards me and not the end of the trial during dark periods. And you know what, sometimes it was and still is another train! However, there is still value in those barreling trains even when they hit us in the dark while we are searching for the light.

So ... what can we learn from the Gethsemane passages? We are not Jesus, after all! It is not as easy for us to tell God, "Not my will but your will be done." Trust me, I understand that truth as much as anyone. However, there are still valuable lessons for the spiritual battles we face that can be invaluable to us today from what Jesus lived out before the disciples. We must look and learn in ways that may be unexpected.

We will not look in an in-depth manner at each account in the Gospels. However, there are moments in each narrative that allow us to see Jesus' own spiritual battle in a light that perhaps has never been seen before. These moments deserve a look because they will provide us with strength and tools for our own journey in the days ahead ... and we will have our days ahead that will need encouragement that only Jesus can provide.

---

[26] The phrase "dark night of the soul" is from the words of the 16th-century Christian mystic St. John of the Cross.

Meaning of Gethsemane

The actual word Gethsemane in Aramaic means "oil press."[27] Hence, Gethsemane is loaded with meaning and irony if one considers the nuances of all that lies behind the word. Olive oil was used to anoint kings, as was the case with Jesus' ancestors, David and Solomon. David was a lowly shepherd who would have to wait years before he ascended to his rightful throne, and his son would almost immediately follow him after David's death, to massive amounts of pomp and ceremony. Olive oil is used in Scripture as a symbol for healing, as mentioned in the book of James, when one would ask the elders to visit the sick. Olive oil was used as a means to dispel the darkness. Obviously, olive oil was also used for cooking – especially for baking bread, which was necessary for survival. Four uses of olive oil, which I would argue are loaded with nuances that also tie themselves back to the person of who Jesus was and is.

However, it is the preparation of this small fruit to become oil that is especially insightful in this chapter's illustration, as this is where Jesus spent his last night of freedom before the cross … at the symbolic olive press of Gethsemane. To prepare olive oil, an individual must first crush or break the flesh of the fruit to allow for the release of the oil from what was once its "fruity container." Additionally, it is worth noting that in biblical times, a millstone was one of the most common tools used for crushing. The remains of the olives were then placed in what I imagine were mesh bags and subjected to immense pressure to release any additional oil that might be left in the olive remains.[28] Therefore, the location for Jesus' encounter with God to ask for release and ultimately acknowledgment of God's will can be equated with being crushed and pressured. I told you there was dramatic irony in this location!

Consequently, and this is important for us as we look more deeply into these passages, sometimes it is in those moments of deepest pain that our deepest triumphs are most often revealed. Yes, Jesus was crushed and pressured as olive oil must also be but he was and will be anointed (think Phil. 2:5-11) as King of Kings and Lord of Lords. If not for the pain of Gethsemane and Golgotha, the victory of the Mount of Olives and the Second Coming is not possible … for any of us. Therefore, we cannot run from our pressure-

---

[27] Emmet Russell, "Gethsemane," *Zondervan's Pictorial Bible Dictionary*, gen. ed. Merrill C. Tenney (Grand Rapids: Zondervan Publishing House, 1967), 310.

[28] "Oil: Extracted by Presses," available online at **https://biblehub.com/topical/ttt/o/oil--extracted_by_presses.htm**; accessed 3 February 2025. Incidentally, I "googled" the question as to whether olives were fruits or vegetables and was surprised by the answer. I always considered them as a vegetable myself.

filled moments (aka "spiritual warfare) because we will then miss our victory moments. Jesus did not pass the cup, and neither must we.

Glancing at the Matthew 26 Passage

In the next chapter, we will consider the temptation accounts in Matthew, Mark, and Luke; however, I believe it would be foolhardy to imagine that Satan was not in Gethsemane, tempting Jesus to give it all up before the soldiers arrived, along with his disciple Judas.[29] In fact, one of my favorite scenes in the film *The Passion of the Christ* was at the beginning of the movie, where we see Jesus crushing the head of the serpent in the garden, foreshadowing the ultimate fulfillment of Genesis 3:15 the next day at Golgotha. However, and in that same scene, we see Satan delivering his final temptation – suggesting that God did not care about Jesus because if God did care, the cross could be avoided.

I can imagine that Satan was there in the garden urging Jesus to walk away from "tomorrow's agony." Telling Jesus that it can all be over if he walks away from the garden and the cross and those sleeping disciples. Indeed, as we see in the passage, there were three requests from Jesus to God the Father for any other way except the cross, and also three self-acknowledgments by Jesus that he would follow the plan (which had been established before time began – Ephesians 2). For Jesus' pain, fear, and sorrow (v. 37-38) were a real expression of his humanity that we often seem to forget or ignore. Wishing for a reprieve was not a sign of weakness on Jesus' part but something that we can hold onto as well. This Matthew passage shows that Jesus understands. Gethsemane reveals that we can go to him when we are at the end of our rope and we simply just want to walk away from the spiritual warfare and the pain of it all (Hebrews 4:14-16). Truly, Jesus understands where we are because he has been there as well. He did not walk away, and because of this truth … neither should we.

Glancing at the Mark 14 Passage

Larry Hurtado, for his commentary on the Gospel of Mark, draws a parallel between Jesus' words in Mark 14:34 to the words of Psalm 42:6a – *"O my God, my soul is cast down within me…"* and to all the verses of Psalm 42.[30] This allusion is especially evident in Psalm 42:9 when one reads the words – *"I will say unto God my rock, Why hast thou forgotten me? why go I mourning because of the oppression of the enemy?"* Therefore, and if

---

[29] Robert H. Mounce, *Matthew*, New International Biblical Commentary, vol. 1, NT ed., W. Ward Gasque (Peabody, MA: Hendrickson Publishers, 1991), 243.

[30] Larry W. Hurtado, *Mark*, New International Bible Commentary, vol. 2, NT ed., W. Ward Gasque (Peabody, MA: Hendrickson Publishers, 1991), 245.

Jesus perhaps did have these words in his heart or mouth as he prayed in Gethsemane that night, I hope we all will have a different consideration in our mind when we next sing Psalm 42:1 – *"As the deer panteth for the water, so my soul longeth after thee..."*

But ... what did it mean for Jesus to say that his soul was sorrowful unto death? Yes, it is again a description of Jesus' humanity, but I believe it is something more than perhaps what we see in a cursory reading of Mark's verses. In Matthew's account, along with the Mark account, we see Jesus telling Peter, James, and John to stay awake and pray in the Greek imperative (command). However, there is almost a sense of a plea here, with the words – "My soul is sorrowful unto death." What could it all mean?

By the understanding of some, Mark wrote his Gospel based on Peter's sharing of his experiences as a disciple of the Messiah.[31] Even though we cannot be certain as to the identity of Mark (see fn. 6), I hold to the view that Peter shared his account of the years with Jesus with Mark, and then he wrote it down under the inspiration of the Holy Spirit. Therefore, we can only imagine what Peter must have felt in hindsight as he recalled Jesus' words and his appeal to those three men who had seen so much, urging them to stay awake with him when he desperately needed not to feel alone. We can only imagine perhaps the guilt Peter felt knowing that he had failed Jesus in Gethsemane, along with the memory of the three denials that more than likely never left Peter's memory – even knowing that he had been forgiven.

Yes ... Jesus felt utterly alone in Gethsemane. His disciples were asleep. Satan must have been in his ear, reminding him of what awaited him on the cross and before the crowd who had at one time cheered him and would soon jeer him. No one could face what Jesus had to face for us but Jesus ... alone. Yet he did it, and there is a lesson for us today as well.

Spiritual warfare is often a battle we must face alone as well. We can have prayer partners. We can have accountability partners. We can have allies in the faith, but the battle is something we must face alone. No one can fight it for us but ourselves – **and the one who fought the greatest battle of all eternity** – the one for our souls. Jesus went through Gethsemane alone so that we can fight our spiritual battles with him by our side – alone but not completely alone.

---

[31] Henry E. Turlington, *Mark*, The Broadman Bible Commentary, vol. 8, gen. ed. Clifton J. Allen (Nashville, TN: Broadman Press, 1969), 255-57, 386-87. It should be noted that there is a great deal of speculation (i.e., guessing as to who Mark was – including identifying him as the cousin of Barnabas), but the identity of the author of Mark cannot be ascertained with 100% certainty.

Glancing at the Luke 22 Passage

As I write parts of this section on Luke 22, I am not having a good day, let alone a good week. It is a period of silence from what feels like God … and from others whom I have grown to depend upon for encouragement. It should be noted that I am learning not to rely on people for spiritual encouragement, as they can let you down – even if they do not intend to do so.

It is also a day when other people seem to need something from me and do not realize that perhaps I am not always in top spirits – sometimes I am being asked to fake it until I can make it. For at the present moment, I am tired. I am lonely. And if I am honest with you … I am a little depressed. Yes … missionaries get depressed from time to time.

Perhaps this is then the perfect time for me to write this section (and this chapter) regarding the warfare and the spiritual battle that Jesus experienced at Gethsemane. I can perhaps see more clearly (if only slightly) a little of what Jesus felt as he waited for Judas to arrive and for "IT" to all begin. The loneliness and sense of isolation are among those expressions of spiritual warfare that we often prefer not to confront. However, they are a very real reality that must be acknowledged not only for our spiritual growth but also so that we will not be overwhelmed by "it" the next time loneliness and isolation appear on our doorstep.

The Luke account (which is also mentioned in Matthew and Mark) focuses on the idea of a cup and Jesus asking for this vessel to be removed from him (v. 42). However, the concept of a cup from our perspective usually goes back to the Upper Room and the phrase the "Holy Grail." Movies have been made, including a very inappropriate one involving Monty Python. Books have been written and battles during the Middle Ages have been fought over supposed sacred relics related to the final days of Jesus' life – including the cup from which Jesus drank while he observed Passover with his disciples.[32]

Yet, it is the Gethsemane cup that is especially significant for all of humanity. The understanding of this cup in a Hebrew spiritual context is related

---

[32] "What Is the Holy Grail – And Where Is It?," available online at **https://earlychurchhistory.org/christian-symbols/what-is-the-holy-grail-and-where-is-it/**; accessed 14 February 2025. I do not hold much stock in the idea of sacred relics still existing 2,000 years after the death and resurrection of Jesus. If such a wooden cup was preserved for any period after the Ascension, it has long disappeared with time and corrosion over the millennia.

to the sense of destiny (Psalm 16:5; Jer. 25:15).[33] Jesus knew that his destiny was to suffer (Is. 52:13-53:12) for the forgiveness of sins of the world and that his suffering would be great. This is why Jesus asked in the imperative sense for it to be taken away, but ... (and also in the imperative sense) he stated, "your will be done." Jesus rejected his temporary human fear and took on his destiny for the greater need of all humanity. This is an amazing gift for us all and a far greater cup than anything that might be called the "Holy Grail," which, more likely than not, has disintegrated over time.

So ... the question we must ask ourselves is simply, are we willing to face our destiny, even if it includes our cup of suffering? Are we willing to face the hour that we might sweat great drops of blood when the hour is long and our friends are asleep at the proverbial wheel?[34] Are we willing to say "not my will, but your will" when God's destiny for our lives just might require suffering that appears to be unimaginable? It should be noted that this does not necessarily mean martyrdom, but rather something that we could never have imagined or desired. Are we willing to face whatever, whenever, and however because God will be glorified? Jesus did for our eternal salvation.

Glancing at the John 18 Passage

Did you notice in the Luke passage that I mentioned that Jesus was waiting for Judas to arrive at Gethsemane and for "IT" to all begin? The John

---

[33] Craig A. Evans, *Luke*, New International Biblical Commentary, vol. 3, NT ed., W. Ward Gasque (Peabody, MA: Hendrickson Publishers, 1990), 329; and Amy-Jill Levine, "Introduction and Annotations for the Gospel of Luke," *The Jewish Annotated New Testament* (NRSV), eds. Amy-Jill Levine and Marc Zvi Brettler (New York: Oxford University Press, 2011), 146. I utilize this particular Study Bible for its uniqueness in that it is a New Testament edited and annotated by Jewish scholars who do not believe in Jesus as Messiah ... yet acknowledge the uniqueness the truth of the New Testament story.

[34] The question might be asked of you at some time in the future – can someone really sweat blood? I believe Jesus did because the Bible says but it is also medically provable. Dave Miller, "Hematidrosis: Did Jesus Sweat Blood?," *Reason & Revelation* (July 2017), available online at **https://apologeticspress.org/hematidrosis-did-jesus-sweat-blood-5436/**; accessed 14 February 2025; Nayana Ambardekar, MD, "What Is Hematidrosis?," available online at **https://www.webmd.com/a-to-z-guides/hematidrosis-hematohidrosis**; accessed 14 February 2025; and "Hematidrosis (Blood in Sweat)," International Hyperhidrosis Society; available online at **https://sweathelp.org/home/hematidrosis-blood-in-sweat.html**; accessed 14 February 2025. Sweating blood most often occurs according to the noted sources when one is under extreme stress and as one of them noted when one is in a "flight or fight" situation.

18 passage, related to Gethsemane, focuses solely on Judas' arrival and the "IT" to begin. There are many reasons for John's "cut to the chase" approach to the Gethsemane story. Matthew, Mark, and Luke are known as the synoptic Gospels, and they approach the life of Jesus from a "kingdom of Heaven (God)" perspective, as J. Ramsey Michaels explains it.[35] In other words, the first three Gospels build up to the revelation of Jesus as not only Messiah but also deity (God), but John spells it out theologically from the very first verses – "In the beginning was the Word…" and continues the theme with the "I Am" statements throughout.[36] One of my former seminary professors, E. Earle Ellis, wrote the following:

> For John, it is the historical character of the event that gives meaning and substance to his theological interpretations. This is the essence of his affirmation that the Word of God became incarnate in Jesus of Nazareth. And this is the nature of the "incarnation" theology that undergirds the whole of John's presentation and distinguishes it from the myths of the Greek religions.[37]

So … John did not spend time with Jesus' time in Gethsemane because he wanted to get to the point of the "horrible" but ultimately glorious weekend. There should be no speculation that John skipped his act of sleeping while Jesus prayed for to do so is to read into the text and this tendency should be avoided in understanding the text and the point.

Therefore, I notice two key points that we can take away from these two verses in John 18, and they are both important. The first is that Judas knew where to find Jesus. In fact, the word "knew" is in a rare tense (pluperfect) in the Greek. This tense is difficult to define and explain, but I am going to put it into my own words if that is allowed … Judas "knew" where to find Jesus because it was destiny for them to encounter each other there at that spot and at that time. This "Amy's explanation of the pluperfect" ties into the second clue … Jesus could have broken with tradition and gone somewhere else to pray, but he chose not to do so because it was time for the crucifixion, and he

---

[35] J. Ramsey Michaels, *John*, New International Biblical Commentary (vol. 4), NT ed., W. Ward Gasque (Peabody, MA: Hendrickson Publishers, 1989), 12-13.

[36] Ibid., 13. I wish there were space to explain the theological significance of the "I Am" statements of John but if there was any question as to whether Jesus proclaimed his divinity – the *ego eimi* ("I Am") proclamations clearly define that Jesus knew who he was and is.

[37] E. Earle Ellis, *The World of St. John: The Gospel and the Epistles* (Lanham, MD: University Press of America, 1995), 52.

did not avoid what lay before him. Jesus faced his destiny even as he prayed what he prayed in Matthew, Mark, and Luke.

We can and must learn this lesson as well. Avoiding our spiritual destiny (even our spiritual warfare) will not change its reality or arrival. I have been there several times in my life when I tried to develop scenarios in which the battle could be avoided, but it always had to be fought. And the delay in facing the spiritual battle only resulted in more pain, more hurt, and more scars that perhaps could have been prevented if I had just "bit the bullet" and confronted the issue when it first reared its ugly head. By the way, I am thinking of a particular example as I am writing this paragraph but I hesitate to spell it out to you in case the people in question read the book and get angry with me all over again. Sigh… Even now, I just do not want to engage.

As I close this chapter, I acknowledge once again this truth – there is no escape from spiritual warfare. Another truth that I must affirm – there is real emotion experienced in spiritual warfare. However, and just like Jesus, we must go through our "dark night(s) of the soul to reach the end of our journey.

This is the life of a Christian – battles, scars, sometimes broken fellowships, oftentimes a lot of joy, defeats, sorrows, and moments of complete ecstasy until we reach Heaven. But … the journey is worth it because Jesus will meet us there and He is with us through every step of our difficult sojourn until we reach those gates that we long to see.

Questions for Individual or Group Study

1.   Without giving into the tendency to give a "Sunday School Answer," what is your human response to the idea – **We need to realize that as a believer in Jesus, there is no escaping from the truth and the reality that there are real emotional components to spiritual warfare. For even though we might and sometimes not be able to see the end of spiritual warfare even while we are going through it, we often still have to go "through the dark night of our soul," to reach the end of it. There is value in these experiences even when we are desperate to escape them at the moment.**

2.   Have you ever considered the location of Gethsemane as significant, given that the name itself means "oil press"? What is your reaction to the idea that in our moments of deepest pain, we often will discover our deepest triumphs? Are you willing to go through pain to discover triumph? Why or why not?

3.   The idea of Jesus experiencing the feeling of loneliness, perhaps, is something that you have not considered before. What is your reaction to this concept? What do you do when you feel lonely? Depressed? Afraid? Is your

reaction to these feelings healthy and/or biblical? Or ... is it something that you need to consider from a different perspective?

4.   Given all that Jesus did for us, including facing his destiny (his cup of suffering) at Gethsemane, is there a limit to what we will do for him if he asks? Be careful before you casually answer this question ... because you never know what Jesus will ask of you. Would you be willing to sacrifice a spouse, a child, a home, or yourself if Jesus asked it of you? Is there a limit to what you might give Jesus in your spiritual growth (warfare)?

5.   Have you ever tried to avoid a spiritual battle only to have to fight the same fight later on that was "bloodier" and longer in engagement than if you had just confronted it earlier in your life? Why do we do this to ourselves? Why do we engage in appeasement when spiritual confrontation is perhaps the better answer?

7

Spiritual Warfare is Often Followed by Great Trials
to Show Us Whether We Truly Trust God
(Matthew 4:1-11; Mark 1:12, 13; Luke 4:1-13)

We might not like it, but we must face the truth that great spiritual victories are often followed by periods of intense spiritual warfare. This is to demonstrate our fidelity and loyalty, or to guide us to the next step in our spiritual growth.

If you grow up in Texas for most of your life, it is almost impossible not to love football. It is part of the DNA of Texas life. Thursday night is reserved for football games for Junior High teams and/or Junior Varsity at the high school level. Friday night is varsity football – especially for small-town life. Pep rallies to cheer the teams to victory. Banners for the team to run through as they take the field. Marching bands, pep squads, cheerleaders, twirlers, flag teams, drill teams, and any version of a cheering team that you can imagine, including what I just mentioned, are created to rally the football team to victory. Football is the mainstay of small-town life in Texas, whether it is 6-man, 8-man, or 11-man football, and when a town grows too small to have football, the town dies, for what else is there to live for on a Friday night. If you doubt me … go to West Texas and drive through the ghost town of McCaulley, and you will see what happened when football left.

And lest I forget … college football and the plethora of teams one can root for across the state of Texas. Families can be divided over Texas vs. Texas A&M, Baylor vs. TCU, and the University of Texas vs. any other team in the state. My family experienced such a division because my daddy's family were University of Texas Longhorn fans, and my mama's family cheered on the Aggies of Texas A&M. Thanksgiving for many years was divided when it came to game time, especially if we hadn't finished eating dinner at one house or the other.

And, of course, there was Sunday afternoon or Monday night football with Howard Cosell and former Dallas Cowboy quarterback "Dandy" Don Meredith. In case you were wondering, we were a Cowboys house, but we also loved the Houston Oilers – especially when Longhorn running back Earl Campbell played for them. Roger Staubach, Tony Dorsett, Drew Pearson, Randy White, and Cliff Harris of the 1970s, when they won two Super Bowls and should have won three if Jackie Smith had not dropped that touchdown in the endzone in Super Bowl XIII. Troy Aikman, Emmitt Smith, Michael Irvin, Deion Sanders, and Charles Haley, when they won three Super Bowls in four years, and should have won more if not for Jerry Jones allowing his ego to get in the way when he fired Jimmie Johnson.

Yes, Texas females are allowed to love their football and I love my Cowboys, my Texas Longhorns, and my favorite high school team – the Bronte Longhorns in West Texas. Jim McKay's opening introduction for the "Wide World of Sports" (1961-1998) – "The thrill of victory, the agony of defeat" could be defined by the emotions one can feel under the lights of any football stadium in Texas. And for me, who has waited and continues to wait and wait and wait for my Dallas Cowboys to reach the heights of glory ever since their last appearance in SB XXX (1996) … the agony of defeat is very, very real. Yes, I am a bit of a fanatic about my Dallas Cowboys.

Yet … the Christian life and its victories are often accompanied by even greater moments of defeat and valleys that bring us to our knees in despair. And … Jesus went through his own moment of triumph during his baptism experience with John the Baptizer, only to be taken immediately to forty days of temptation, loneliness, and deprivation (i.e., spiritual warfare) in the wilderness. We see Jesus' encounter with warfare and Satan in the Synoptic Gospels (Matthew, Mark, Luke), not just to see that he defeated Satan, but also as a template for how we can be victors as well. And from what I see, we might win this victory before the Cowboys ever win another Super Bowl. Sigh!

Reflections on the Temptations from the Synoptic Gospels

In his commentary on Matthew, Frank Stagg writes something succinct but also profound about Jesus' temptation in the wilderness: "The temptations of Jesus are to be taken at face value. They were not sham battles but real struggles. They probably reflect not so much uncertainty of mind as a test of will."[38] I realize that we all more than likely have heard sermons about how Jesus' temptations reflect what John wrote about 1 John 2:16 – "…the lust of the flesh, the lust of the eyes, and the pride of life…" Perhaps there is some truth to this statement; however, I cannot help but wonder if there was something more to Jesus' temptations than just lust and pride – especially given the timing of Jesus' temptation.

All three of the Gospels show that Jesus went from the closeness of baptism – a Trinitarian experience if there ever was one[39] – to the loneliness of the wilderness. As I mentioned earlier, this is often the scenario for many of us

---

[38] Frank Stagg, *Matthew*, The Broadman Bible Commentary, vol. 8, gen. ed. Clifton J. Allen (Nashville, TN: Broadman Press, 1969), 96.

[39] God the Father spoke, God the Son was baptized, and God the Holy Spirit descended as a dove.

in our Christian lives: a moment of joy and victory followed by doubt and questioning whether we are good enough to serve God.

The legendary 19th-century British pastor Charles Spurgeon is perhaps the best example that comes to mind when one considers the internal struggle that many experience in this battle of feeling unworthy of the high calling we are asked to undertake.[40] He once said of himself: "I cannot yet call myself free from fits of deep depression, which are the result of brain-weariness; but I am having them less frequently, and therefore I hope they will vanish altogether."[41] Those moments of depression never did vanish from Spurgeon's life, and neither did they leave Mother Teresa, who lived a life full of anguish or what she called the silence of God.[42]

And while Jesus experienced temptation so that he could understand our suffering and so that he could become the perfect atoning sacrifice (Heb. 4:14-16), I also believe there was a secondary purpose to this initial temptation account that we find in Matthew, Mark, and Luke – a template for how we can overcome the temptation to walk away from our ultimate Christian purpose. Frank Stagg also expressed this thought even while describing the overarching nature of Jesus' temptation: "[it was] to take a short-cut to immediate goals yielding real benefactions or to employ the wrong means to achieve goals which at least in part represented valid human needs."[43] For while only a masochist seeks out spiritual warfare, a spiritual warrior for God understands it is for our good, our growth, and God's ultimate cause that spiritual warfare comes to our neighborhood. It is a tool to measure our loyalty, our fidelity, and sometimes to move us along to the next growth step of our Christian walk.

And ... I can already hear the Bible pages turning because some of you, many of you, should be asking, does God then tempt us to sin? **And the answer is a big giant – NO!** Scripture is clear on this matter – *"Let no man say when he is tempted, I am tempted of God: for God cannot be tempted with evil, neither tempteth he any man: But every man is*

---

[40] Mitchel Pierce, "Charles Haddon Spurgeon on Depression," Whitworth University 2018), *History of Christianity II: TH 314*, Paper 19, available online at **https://digitalcommons.whitworth.edu/th314h/19**; accessed 24 February 2025.

[41] Ibid.

[42] Brian Kolodiejchuk and Mother Teresa, *Mother Teresa: Come Be My Light – The Private Writings of the Saint of Calcutta* (New York: Random House/Image, 2009). The whole book is fascinating and heartbreaking and regardless if one is Catholic or not, the book should be read for those who are interested in the topic of depression and suffering experienced by Christians.

[43] Stagg, *Matthew*, 97.

tempted, when he is drawn away of his own lust, and enticed. Then when lust hath conceived, it bringeth forth sin: and sin, when it is finished, bringeth forth death" (James 1:13-15). Additionally, 1 Corinthians 10:13 tells us the same message along with the promise that we will not have to endure more than we can endure IF we turn to God to help us escape – *"There hath no temptation taken you but such as is common to man: but God is faithful, who will not suffer you to be tempted above that ye are able; but will with the temptation also make a way to escape, that ye may be able to bear it."*

I want to be clear on this matter that temptation does not come from God. We can be examined/tested/studied by God at the height of our spiritual warfare, but we will not be tempted to sin. Do not blame God for failing if one does ... blame yourself for not finding or looking for the escape hatch that he always provides.

Fasting Question Addendum...

Perhaps I am the only one who has ever asked the question – why was fasting necessary for Jesus? I am someone who cannot fast physically due to health issues, and given that I am a Baptist, I do not usually "give up something for Lent." I did give up Pop-Tarts one time in seminary for Lent, but I'm not sure if that really counts, as I was also trying to lose weight. Therefore, the question of fasting as it relates to Jesus' temptation and our own today is a challenging one to answer.

Examples of fasting are found throughout the Hebrew Scriptures (Old Testament), such as when Queen Esther asked the Jewish people to fast as she prepared to go before the king (Esther 4:16) or when Elijah fled from Jezebel and was in the wilderness (1 Kings 19). Examples are not as common in the New Testament, and even when Jesus mentions fasting, he instructs the people to keep it private between themselves and God (Matthew 6:16-18).

So ... why did Jesus fast in the wilderness? What was its purpose? Should we fast today? I cannot answer the third question for anyone but myself because I simply cannot, or it would harm my health. If anyone who is reading this book chooses to fast, I encourage them to prepare carefully, with a great deal of prayer, and to keep Matthew 6:16-18 in mind while doing so. And with that out of the way, let's answer the questions that need to be answered for this chapter.

Why did Jesus fast in the wilderness, and what was its purpose? Is it because Jesus wanted to emulate the Israelites' time in "The Wilderness" and illustrate that he could, and unlike those annoying former slaves, not fall to temptation and neither doubt God?[44] Norval Geldenhuys believed the purpose of the fasting was because "[t]he conflict with the prince of the forces of darkness demands His attention and powers… The sense of physical need had been supplanted throughout by the violence of the spiritual conflict."[45]

I want to offer a third option, and you can decide which one is the best possibility or perhaps even a combination of the three. Perhaps … the fasting had nothing to do with the temptation that Jesus was experiencing at that moment. Perhaps … the fasting Jesus experienced was in spiritual preparation for what was to come not only in the wilderness also but for all of Jesus' ministry – something we will consider again when we look at Luke 4:13. And with this possible thought in mind, I want to ask you and myself three important questions that still penetrate every time I look at them.

Three Core Questions Related to Spiritual Warfare

The first temptation Jesus faced was the offer to turn stones into bread. Yes, Jesus was hungry after forty days of fasting, but the real question is not the "lust of the flesh" but really what is most important to you – the physical or the spiritual? In other words, does someone wish to fulfill their human desires/needs or their spiritual ones?

This has become a very real issue in today's world. We live in a visual society. We are trained to fulfill what our eyes see and want. Pornography today is not found under a teenage boy's mattress anymore, but on the darkest parts of the internet at a moment's notice, and it is vastly worse than whatever *Playboy* could produce. I once heard the atheist Bill Maher say that no one could be expected to abstain from sex anymore because we cannot control ourselves. Is anyone single and a virgin anymore?

Yes, you are reading her book. Has it always been easy? Definitely, not. Yet … what is most important to my life – the spiritual or the physical? The living stone or the moldy bread? I could go on, but I believe you understand the point I am trying to make. And this is the point that needs to be made not just to the church's "young people" (as we tend to fixate on young people and

---

[44] E. Earle Ellis, *The Gospel of Luke*, The New Century Bible Commentary, NT ed. Matthew Black (Grand Rapids, MI: William B. Eerdmans, 1996 rprt.), 96. As I mentioned in an earlier chapter, Dr. Ellis was one of my seminary professors and I have the utmost respect and admiration for him. My inclusion of the phrase "annoying Hebrew slaves" was mine and mine alone.

[45] Norval Geldenhuys, *Commentary on the Gospel of Luke*, The New International Commentary on the New Testament, gen. ed. F. F. Bruce (Grand Rapids: William B. Eerdmans, 1975 rprt.), 196.

sex), because this issue in our spiritual welfare discipleship is perhaps one of the hardest of them all.

The second temptation boils down to the question (Matthew 4:5-7) – do you trust God enough? When the whole world is daring you to throw it all away on a dare (i.e., prove that your God is big enough), do we trust God to remain silent and unmovable in the face of the doubters? This is often harder than we might think, and one that I frequently fail at myself, but it is one that we must learn to overcome.

I remember that one of my former students at the small Bible college in Texas came to me one day with a question he struggled to answer from a former high school friend who had become an agnostic since they last saw each other. The question was one that is common in the agnostic world, but "Drew" was stumped – "Can God create a rock so big that he can not lift it?"

His agnostic friend challenged him with this question because he knew that Drew believed God created everything and believed God was all-powerful (omniscient). So, can God create a rock so big that even God Himself could not lift it? This was something that Drew was struggling to answer. I looked at Drew and asked him one question – **"Why would God need to create such a rock?"**

Drew started laughing and realized that the question was all about trust. His friend was challenging his trust in God just as Satan was daring Jesus in the Wilderness. Jesus passed the test because he quoted Scripture, something that we lack the knowledge to do in this day and age. However, it is more than just our "Bible Sword" knowledge. The real question is – do we trust God in our wilderness times?

Do we trust God when we are hungry and thirsty and teetering on the precipice? Do we trust God when it is dark and lonely and the test results from the doctor are the worst possible news? Do we trust God when our checking account is quickly heading towards zero and the calendar is still not at the end of the month?

A few months after I answered Drew's question, I was greeted by the Academic Dean of this small "Christian" college with the news that I was being non-renewed (i.e., fired) at the end of the academic year. No reason was given for this decision – although I had the highest student-teacher evaluation scores and was the only professor to be published. The only reason I could imagine was that I had been warned that I was not a "team player" because I would give the athletes the grades they had earned, which meant they would be ineligible to play the next semester.

Yes, I panicked and even found myself panicking in the middle of the grocery store the next week because I had just bought a house and moved my mama in with me to help her live out the last few years of her life in comfort. I was trying to figure out how to pay the mortgage and cover groceries in the middle of the vegetable aisle, not just for the next month, but for the next few months, all at the same time. My mama found me melting down next to the green beans and reminded me that it was going to be alright and that God was bigger than a small Baptist college that put baseball ahead of integrity. And, indeed, God provided in unexpected ways. Ways that allowed me to go full-time as a missionary to the Jewish people. Ways that ensured we never missed a mortgage payment and always had more than enough green beans on our table. Because mama (more than I) trusted God enough.

If I were going to summarize the third and final temptation (Matthew 4:8-10), I would describe it as Satan saying to Jesus, "God gives you the cross and I can give you the world." This was the point of Satan bringing Jesus to what was, in essence, the "top of the world" in verse 8. Obviously, Jesus chose the cross, but we miss something in the English translation in verse 9 because what Satan wanted was not just a one-time bowing of the knee but eternal submission of God the Son.

The verb "fall down" is an aorist active participle that indicates an action in progress. The verb for worship is an aorist active subjunctive, again conveying the sense of ongoing action. Satan wanted to own or "control" Jesus – just like he does us. This is why the words of Jesus when he banished Satan are so important. For while Jesus quoted scripture, and this is for our benefit more than his own, Jesus was also imperative in his instruction to depart. Don't suggest that Satan leave. Be strong!

For the question that will often trouble at the back of our minds – regardless of whether you admit it or not – is who will you worship when it all craters in on you? I will admit that I have been tempted to throw it all away and run to the world where it was easier … or appeared to be easier. The pains, the losses, and the hurts of being in ministry can bring even the strongest person to their knees and I am not as strong as I should be if I am honest with you. I want to be stronger. I work on my walk with God every day, but I have my moments of weakness. And it is in those weak moments, those cratering moments, that I hear the voice whispering, "Is it worth it? Just walk away. The world is so much more fun and easier."

It is also those moments that I have to commit myself to worship God and serve him only – even in the darkest and deepest craters. For as Corrie ten Boom reminds us – "There is no pit so deep that God is not deeper still."

Now and before we close this most difficult of chapters for me to write, and perhaps for you to read, I want to remind you of Luke 4:13b. The King James uses the phrase, "he [Satan] departed him for a season." Other versions use the phrase "until an opportune time." This illustrates to us that

Satan did not leave Jesus alone, and he will not leave us alone. Temptation is just around the corner, waiting to catch us unaware and unprepared.

This angle of spiritual warfare is unfair from the human perspective. When we are weak, it pounces, and we will talk more about that fact in the next chapter. When we are vulnerable, it is ready to claim another victim. That is why this chapter is so important to our spiritual discipleship. The demon is not under every rock, but temptation is, and we must be ready for when it attacks. This is not encouraging news, is it? But it is truthful.

Questions for Individual or Group Study

1.   Without giving into the tendency to give a "Sunday School Answer," what is your human response to the idea – **We might not like it, but we must face the truth that great spiritual victories are often followed by periods of intense spiritual warfare. This is to demonstrate our fidelity and loyalty, or to guide us to the next step in our spiritual growth.**

2.   Have you ever been "tempted" to take shortcuts in your discipleship path by avoiding the difficult route of spiritual battles? If you have done so, what spiritual lesson do you think you avoided learning in the so-called shortcut? Would you go back and take the more difficult journey if you could repeat it? Why or why not?

3.   What is your view on fasting? Have you ever abstained from something for any length of time to draw closer to God? Did you find it difficult or impossible to finish your fast? Did you find the desire to give in to what you had given up was a temptation that you had never experienced before? Why do you think that was?

4.   What is your "spiritual vs. physical" issue? Food? Finances? Purity – in whatever version it is presented? Something else? We all have one and we all have to give it over to God or we will eat the moldy bread instead of turning to the living stone when we are weak.

5.   Trusting God in the middle of plenty is easy. Trusting God in the middle of want is much harder. How do you trust God when trust seems impossible? Do you find it difficult to trust God enough? What do you need to do to improve your trust level?

8

Spiritual Warfare Is Often About Survival and Surrender
(1 Peter 5:6-10)

We need to acknowledge that surviving spiritual warfare involves surrendering control of ourselves and allowing ourselves to be humbled by the ONE who can control all of life's surprises.

I began my first semester at Southwestern Baptist Theological Seminary in the fall of 1993. However, it should be noted that I was still in my resistance phase, as it relates to serving God wholeheartedly, even during my first seminary years. I knew that I was called to full-time service, but … I was bound and determined that I would not be a missionary. I would find a way to serve God, but I was going to do it in my own way. Yeah … that obviously worked out well. Trust me that never works, for as the old cliché states, "Man plans and God laughs," always comes true.

God began laughing at me even during my first seminary course which was a book study on Peter's first epistle to the scattered believers "throughout Pontus, Galatia, Cappadocia, Asia, and Bithynia." (1 Peter 1:1b). The professor was the Greek scholar Curtis Vaughan who was able to bring the words of the apostle to life even on a Monday night in a crowded and occasionally stuffy classroom in a way that I have never seen before or since. In fact, I will share an account that Dr. Vaughan shared from the last night of the course as we examine verse 5:10 in the final words of this chapter – an account that brought everyone in the classroom to tears.

However, any study of 1 Peter must include an understanding of two issues: (1) who were the aliens/strangers of 1:1 and (2) what was the nature of the suffering being experienced by those individuals to whom Peter was writing? The aliens/strangers "scattered" as it is written in the KJV, NIV, and the NASB is also translated in other versions with the phrase "of the Dispersion" (NKJV, RSV, ASV, DBY, ESV). The reason for the different renderings in English is that the word Peter used in Greek is *Diaspora*. And … if that word looks familiar, it is because it is most often used to describe the "scattering" of the Jewish people throughout history – from Babylon in 586 BC/BCE to when the Romans destroyed Jerusalem in AD/CE 70.[46]

So … is this possibly a clue as to the identity of the primary audience of Peter's letter in the first century? Let's go on to consider additional clues that might answer the question. Galatians 2:8, which is another account of the Jerusalem Council that can also be found in Acts 15, tells us the following – *"(For he that wrought effectually in Peter to the apostleship of the circumcision, the same was mighty in me toward the Gentiles:)."* It should not be inferred that Peter only shared the Gospel with Jewish people, as is evident from the message shared in Acts 10. However, while Paul primarily focused on reaching out to Gentile people, Peter focused primarily on reaching out to Jewish people scattered throughout the Roman Empire.[47]

So … with the first question out of the way, let us consider the nature of the suffering being experienced by the Jewish believers in Asia Minor. Given that I affirm Peter was the author of the letter, the epistle was written before AD/CE 64, indicating that the suffering occurred before the empire-authorized persecution under Nero.[48] Therefore, it was localized and by their neighbors and perhaps former friends, making it more personal and, dare I say, more real.

Claudia Setzer, writing as a contributor to the Jewish Annotated New Testament, does an excellent job of fusing the nature of the persecution experienced by Jewish believers in Asia Minor into three or four accusations that would make us laugh today, but were very real charges in the first century. Accusations such as false worship and/or being atheists (since they only

---

[46] Kenneth S. Wuest, *First Peter in the Greek New Testament for the English Reader* (Grand Rapids: William B. Eerdmans, 1945), 13-15. See also, Norman Hillyer, *1 and 2 Peter, Jude*, New International Biblical Commentary, vol. 16, NT ed. W. Ward Gasque (Peabody, MA: Hendrickson Publishers, 1992), 3-4, 26. Interestingly, Hillyer admits that the word *Diaspora* is a term that is used for the Jewish people but wants to see the audience of 1 Peter as a mixed audience comprised mainly of Gentile believers in Jesus. I personally believe he is wrong and am confused as to why he sees the term as Jewish in context but Gentile in terms of audience makeup.

[47] L. Ann Jervis, *Galatians*, New International Biblical Commentary, vol. 9, NT ed. W. Ward Gasque (Peabody, MA: Hendrickson Publishers, 1992), 57-58. For a more detailed explanation as to why the audience of 1 Peter should be understood as a primarily Jewish audience, see Jim Sibley, "What If Peter Was Writing to the Jews? The Evidence and the Implications," available online at **https://www.oneforisrael.org/bible-based-teaching-from-israel/peter-writing-jews-evidence-implications/**; accessed 11 March 2025.

[48] Hillyer, *1 and 2 Peter, Jude*, 3, 5.

worshipped one God), "hatred of humanity," lack of patriotism since they would not pray or worship Caesar, and engaging in deviant sexual behaviors.[49] Yes, rumors spread throughout the empire that Christians engaged in deviant acts during communion (i.e., the Lord's Supper). Yet, Peter, Paul, and James in their letters told the churches to love, to obey authorities, and to count it all joy when they experienced trials (1 Peter 4:13; James 1:2).

Consequently, as we begin to focus on this chapter, we must recognize that suffering is a component, often a key one, of spiritual warfare. For surviving spiritual warfare and suffering involves surrendering control of ourselves to be humbled to the ONE who can control things – the ONE who should be our best friend. Yes, I repeated the theme of the chapter because I believe it deserves to be repeated … especially as we consider what 1 Peter 5:6-10 has to tell us even when it requires the difficult subject of suffering.

What Does It Mean to Humble Ourselves? (v. 6)

It appears that the 1970s marked the beginning of choruses for many churches and youth groups. If you were alive and survived riding banana-seat bicycles while wearing terry-cloth shirts and bell-bottom corduroys, as I did, you might also remember the classic "Pass It On" that began with the words, "It only takes a spark to get the fire going." If this song is not registering in your mind, then what about the earworm catchy "Soon and Very Soon" by Andrae Crouch or Larry Norman's "I Wish We'd All Been Ready?" Among those songs that are now stuck in my head at the moment was a chorus that was based on James 4:10 – *"Humble yourselves in the sight of the Lord, and he shall lift you up."*[50] The reason I mention this song in relation to 1 Peter 5:6 is not only because the sense of the verse is the same, but also because the message and the Greek are the same. And if Bob Hudson knew Greek, I wonder if he would have written the song in 1979? Consequently, I wonder if many of the songs we sing in church today (both old and new) would have been written if the writers had a sense of the biblical languages or theology, but that is an issue for another day.

Anyway … the word "humble" in James 4:10 and 1 Peter 5:6 has the same meaning – "to bring low" and/or "to be abased" (i.e., subjugated) – and

---

[49] Claudia Setzer, "Introduction and Annotations for 1 Peter," *The Jewish Annotated New Testament* (NRSV), eds. Amy-Jill Levine and Marc Zvi Brettler (New York: Oxford University Press, 2011), 438.

[50] Bob Hudson, "Humble Yourself in the Sight of the Lord," available online at **https://wordtoworship.com/song/9018**; accessed 13 March 2025. Still under copyright – CCLI #26564.

the same Greek tense … an aorist imperative passive.[51] Now, I have mentioned the concept of an imperative before – command. The aorist passive voice is when the action is done to or upon the noun – "the ball hit him." Therefore, when 1 Peter 5:6 tells us to "humble yourself in the sight of the Lord," the understanding is that you **will be** humbled/abased/brought low/subjugated under God's mighty hand **so that** God may/will exalt (lift you up) in his time (*Kairos*). So … do you want to sing that song now?

However, our humbling and/or subjugation are key components in our spiritual growth. In fact, we cannot grow in our relationship with God if we do not first abase/lower ourselves from the lofty perch on which we so often place ourselves. This does not involve self-flagellation as was common during the Middle Ages, which accomplished little but scars on someone's back.[52] Humbling ourselves consists of the self-realization that we can accomplish little in this world under our own ability – especially our growth as believers in Messiah Jesus.

It is God's mighty hand alone that will choose to exalt you in his time. This is the second hard reality … at least for me. God's timing rarely fits within calendar blocks – if ever – and we should be grateful for this truth. His timing (*Kairos*), which is vastly different than our rigid "sands in the hourglass" approach (Kronos), is actually going to be always right on time, for it will occur when we are spiritually ready for the next adventure or the next obstacle that we are scheduled to experience. Hmm … spiritually scheduled to experience? An interesting turn of phrase, even if I just wrote it, but it does describe the reality of spiritual warfare/growth, even I say so myself.

Casting Our Care Upon the Lord (v. 7)

Norman Hillyer points out that 1 Peter 5:7 is a very close translation of the first part of Psalm 55+:22 – "Cast thy burden upon the Lord, and he shall sustain thee: he shall never suffer the righteous to be moved."[53] A verse that Peter's Jewish audience would have known well, regardless of where they lived in the Roman Empire. And even today, we have all heard sermons and Christian platitudes about taking our burdens to the Lord and leaving them there. However, and we should be honest enough to admit it, it is often easier said than done.

---

[51] Wuest, *First Peter in the Greek New Testament for the English Reader*, 128.

[52] Eyewitness to History, "The Flagellants Attempt to Repel the Black Death, 1349," available online at **http://www.eyewitnesstohistory.com/flagellants.htm**; accessed 18 March 2025.

[53] Hillyer, *1 and Peter, Jude*, 145.

This is why I believe that Peter used the Greek word for "casting" in the aorist active participial tense. I know the recent use of Greek might seem excessive, but at the moment, it is necessary. An aorist verb does not always have a past, present, or future tense, so it can be seen as all three, especially since it is in the participle form. We are to cast our burdens … all the time upon the Lord and not just once. Burdens arrive all the time, and we are to cast (transfer our burdens to God) because we acknowledge that we cannot handle the "stuff" that life gives to us anymore.[54]

Kenneth Wuest beautifully explains why we should do this, the handing off of our burdens, when he interprets the phrase "for he careth for you." He writes the following – "…for you are His concern. Anxiety is a self-contradiction to true humility. Unbelief is, in a sense, an exalting of self against God in that one is depending upon self and failing to trust God. Why worry therefore, if we are His concern."[55] Indeed, we are God's concern, and that should fill us with amazing confidence and comfort. These verses of 1 Peter 5:6-7 are the premise of hope as we prepare for the reality of verses 8-9 because the reality of what we are to face is just as frightening as verses 6-7 are balm to our souls.

Don't Let Your Guard Down – You Are Being Watched (v. 8-9)

As a preacher's kid to a Baptist pastor, I know what it means to be watched! People in the community watched me, regardless of whether they attended our church or not. Church members watched me. Deacons and, most definitely, the deacons' wives watched me. The concept of living in a fishbowl is the very definition of being a Baptist preacher's kid. It felt as if I made one slip-up, the U-Haul van could be waiting at the parsonage the following day, waiting for us to load up and move to the next church and the next group of watching eyes. However, the eyes of those deacons' wives are nothing like the eyes of Satan, who is continually seeking (an active participle in this verb) someone(s) he can devour – even if some of those deacons' wives that our family experienced in some Texas churches felt like they were married to you-know-who. Wait … should I have written that last sentence? Yes … definitely leaving the sentence in the final manuscript.

For Satan is our adversary (*antidikos*), a term in Greek that means more than just an opponent, but a term that should bring to mind a challenger/foe in a courtroom setting. Satan wants to destroy everything that makes us who

---

[54] Explanation of the Greek word cast "epiripto" in Bible Hub. Available online at **https://biblehub.com/greek/1977.htm**; accessed 18 March 2025.

[55] Wuest, *First Peter in the Greek New Testament for the English New Testament*, 129.

we are. Again, this is not about the demon under the rock but an out-in-the-open opponent who constantly throws those rocks at us so that we will turn and run from the spiritual battle that must be fought. A fight not only for our spiritual growth but an evangelistic battle for the hearts and souls of the lost.

This is why we are commanded (both aorist imperative verbs) to do two things in verse 8 (KJV) – be sober and be vigilant. We understand the idea of vigilance – do not let your guard down. However, are we careful to be vigilant in our Christian walk? Do we guard our hearts and minds from those issues that can break us down? When I was younger, pastors (including my dad) would call such issues our besetting sins.

The online *Merriam-Webster's Dictionary* defines "besetting sin" as a main or constant problem or fault. One of the online websites that many Christians go to for answers (**www.gotquestions.org**) defines the term as sins "that we continually struggle with and have a weakness toward."[56] And before you say, I don't have any of those issues. Your issue is obviously lying. For we all have a besetting sin, all of us, and those sins are what Satan targets and what we must be vigilant about in our lives.

However, what does the KJV mean by being sober? Is it as simple as not drinking? Well … no and yes to a degree. The word "sober" (*nepho*) originally derived from the idea of "abstaining from wine," but it means more than being a teetotaler. It is the idea of being in control of yourself. In other words, letting go of whatever might cause you to lose control of your spiritual walk. Obviously, and for some, it is alcohol, but for others in this day and age, it could be social media or something else. Whatever causes you not to be **nepho** and therefore not in control … let it go. But not letting go of your weaknesses makes you vulnerable to that roaring lion who wants to consume you.

As we approach verse 9, I want you to know that I am one of those individuals who struggle with allergies. I am severely allergic to mold and will have trouble breathing if black mold is anywhere in the room. In other words, I can be your mold detector if necessary. Pine trees are not my friend, especially in the spring. However, the greatest tragedy is that too much chocolate will cause me to have migraines. And by too much, I mean any more than a small bar of chocolate. However, medical advancements have developed to the point where I can take an antihistamine, fall asleep because all pills make me sleepy,

---

[56] "What Are Besetting Sins?," Got Questions; available online at **https://www.gotquestions.org/besetting-sins.html**; accessed 19 March 2025. Personally, I cannot always recommend this website; however, this is a good explanation of the theological concept. They also provide a scriptural citation of Hebrews 12:1 to explain where the term originated.

and my allergies will be better for a while. However, I still cannot eat too much chocolate, or I will have a migraine, which is tragic!

The reason for sharing all this information is that the word for "resist" (KJV and most other versions) is the word *anthistemi,* which is the purpose of antihistamines. We have histamines in our body that regulate our inflammatory responses to various issues. However, an overload of histamines is what causes an allergic reaction, and why we need an antihistamine.[57] The antihistamine stands up against the histamines that threaten to bring us to our knees (or perhaps a Neti-Pot in my case), and Peter was encouraging the Jewish believers of his day to utilize their faith to stand against the Satanic wiles in their day … a message we need in our day as well. For those wiles (i.e., spiritual histamines) lie within us just waiting to rise and to defeat us when we can least resist.

However, and this should have been a word of encouragement for the recipients of Peter's letter and a word of hope for us as well, we are not alone in the battle. This is the message of v. 9b that Christians around the world are experiencing some level (many far worse than we could ever imagine) of suffering for the name of Messiah Jesus. However, they are resisting/standing firm because they are strong, and so can we. We can stand strong together because we are not alone. We might never see each other or know each other's name because on one level, we are fighting alone; however, in our aloneness, we are not lonely because the Christian family is united by the victory of the Messiah's sacrifice and resurrection for us all.

After You Have Suffered a While (v. 10)

As I was writing this chapter, my former college student Josh, whom I wrote about in *Missions in the Minor Key,* experienced his ultimate healing from a lifetime struggle with Duchenne Muscular Dystrophy. Josh lived a life with as much freedom and happiness as one could. He married and had a son. He graduated from college and was even a youth pastor for a time. He lived his 43 years of life that he was given with as much gusto as possible, given that he spent most of those years from the confines of a wheelchair and in the seventeen years that I knew him, without the use of his arms and hands.

Understand and recognize that Josh experienced low moments in life. He shared those times with me, but Josh knew his suffering and spiritual warfare were only for a little while. He was waiting for the ultimate Independence Day when he would run down the streets of gold and dance

---

[57] Cleveland Clinic, "Histamine," available online at **https://my.clevelandclinic.org/health/articles/24854-histamine**; accessed 19 March 2025. I learned much more about antihistamines than I ever thought possible. Interesting article if you want to learn more about H1 and H2 Receptors.

before the throne of God. And that was why I took advantage of leading those who attended the memorial service in a brief rendition of the "Hokey Pokey" when I spoke the eulogy at his memorial service. For we needed to dance with Josh as he dances in Heaven after being restricted from movement for so long (but even so just a little while) on earth.

And … this idea of a little while is the hope we all can cling to from the words of Peter. For we are called by the God of all grace – what a wonderful phrase Peter crafted for the Jewish believers cast about the Roman Empire and for us as well. Kenneth Wuest describes it simply as an "eternal summons" by the one who offers us "spiritual comfort" for all our needs.[58] But we will also suffer and battle while we are here … sigh!

This was why Dr. Vaughan reminded us on that last night of my 1 Peter seminary course of what verse 10 offered to us in our future ministry endeavors. Yes, we would suffer in the work of Christian service, for that was the promise of the passage, but we would also have the promises of the rest of the verse to cling to when the battle pulled us down to the lowest of the lows. God himself would perfect (complete), confirm, strengthen, and establish us (all future tense verbs).

And as Dr. Vaughan elaborated on this verse with the class, he shared how he clung to verse 10 when his first wife died of cancer. He revealed that during the long nights of his soul, when he thought he would die of grief, he longed for death to take him away from the battles of life. Yet, he knew he had to continue fighting for his family, his faith, and the future that lay before him, perfected, confirmed, strengthened, and established by God himself.

As he was sharing, the class next door, which was a course on Christian Worship, began to sing "Victory in Jesus" almost as if on cue. The 100 students in my 1 Peter class could not hold back the tears as Dr. Vaughan dismissed our class and encouraged us all to stand firm. Stand firm when the bank account has $0.06 and it is only Thursday. Stand firm when a ministry fires us because they can and they do not care. Stand firm because the suffering is only for just a little while.

And as I close this chapter, I want to remind you that holding firm often means letting go of control and allowing ourselves to be humbled by the one who longs to strengthen us one day in a little while. Josh has discovered this reality as he is dancing and running for the first time. We just have to hold on in our battles for that day as well.

---

[58] Wuest, *First Peter in the Greek New Testament for the English Reader*, 130.

Questions for Individual or Group Study

1.   Without giving into the tendency to give a "Sunday School Answer," what is your human response to the idea – **We need to acknowledge that surviving spiritual warfare involves surrendering control of ourselves and allowing ourselves to be humbled by the one who can control all of life's surprises.**

2.   Do you struggle with the thought of allowing yourself to be subjugated/abased/demeaned by God to be used by him? Have you ever considered this definition of "humble yourselves" in such a way? What is your reaction to it? Are you willing to be subjugated if it means that your spiritual growth will flourish as God wants for you?

3.   Do you have a hard time taking your burdens to the Lord and leaving them there? Why or why not? If so, what keeps you from letting go? Is it a control freak mentality? Is it a tendency to perfectionism and a belief that you have to help God out? Is it a fear that if you let go of something, everything will fall apart? What is it, and what must you do to let go and let God?

4.   What is your "besetting sin?" Have you admitted to yourself that you have a besetting sin? What must you do to be ***nepho*** about it so that you will not be vulnerable to the wiles of Satan? Is your besetting sin keeping you from being equipped for the spiritual battle that you must fight today? Why can't you let it go?

5.   Are you loaded up on your "spiritual antihistamines?" If not, what do you need to do to be prepared for those histamines that are waiting to attack when we are weak and susceptible? Does it encourage you to know that you are not alone in this battle, even if you never meet those who are fighting the spiritual warfare with you? Why or why not?

6.   "Just a little while" … Is this a phrase that encourages or discourages you now that you have finished chapter eight? Are you willing to be perfected (completed), confirmed, strengthened, and established (all future tense verbs) by God himself, even if it means that it will not happen until our life is over? Is the spiritual battle worth it, or do you want to run?

Part Two: What Can We Learn About Spiritual Warfare from the Life of Jeremiah?

I mentioned in chapter five that I am much more like the Apostle Paul than I humanly wish to be – too blunt, too caustic, and way too honest at times. I also identify with Jeremiah, who would have been classified as a melancholy-choleric on the dated temperament types we used to take in the 1980s and 1990s, which were supposed to help us identify the kind of career we were suited for and the ideal future spouse.[59] An interesting analogy since Jeremiah was not given the choice of what career he was allowed to pursue and was told he would never marry. Interestingly, two things that I also was not really given a choice about, either if you have read what I have written.

As one reads through Jeremiah and Lamentations, one will see a man filled with angst and sorrow over the spiritual condition of the people he loved. One will find a man not only at the bottom of a well literally but also figuratively for who could not be depressed at times to see Judah descend into spiritual chaos just as the Babylonian horde was approaching. And … sadly there was nothing that the prophet Jeremiah could do to stop it.

The final chapters of this book on spiritual warfare will focus on the life of Jeremiah as he navigated through his life and the final days of Judah/Jerusalem before the arrival of Nebuchadnezzar in 586 BC/BCE. Days in which no one seemingly listened to him. Days in which he ended up in some most unusual places. Days in which more people were against him than for him. And days in which the reality of spiritual warfare was very real and very mucky to say the least.

---

[59] The following is an abbreviated definition of a Melancholy-Choleric according to the "The Fifteen Temperament Blends," available online at **https://fourtemperaments.com/15-temperament-blends/**; accessed 31 March 2025 –

> They not only want to do things right and get results, they strive to figure out what is right… The Melancholy-Choleric is attentive to details and push[es] to have things done correctly according to their standards. They have high standards for themselves and others. They can be a perfectionist about some things."
>
> They are sensitive and conscientious. They can behave in a diplomatic manner, except when it comes to deviating from their standards. The Melancholy-Choleric can be too forceful in insisting the right way (or their way) be followed.

9

Spiritual Warfare Is Often About Being Unpopular
in Today's "Christian World"
(Jeremiah 1:1-10)

**Spiritual warfare often requires us to deliver unpopular messages –
especially when we feel inadequate and must lean on God's power to
accomplish His work.**

When examining the life of Jeremiah, it is essential to start with the
historical setting outlined in verses 1-3. Jeremiah was given his marching orders
during the reign of King Josiah (640-609 BC/BCE), which takes one back to
the final "glory" days of the Southern Kingdom (Judah) as well as the beginning
of its end. Verses 2-3 convey to the readers that Jeremiah was a prophet during
the reign of the last four official kings of Judah, and that he was present during
the destruction of Solomon's Temple and the first Diaspora (dispersion) of the
Jewish people from the land in 586 BC/BCE.

No wonder, then, that Jeremiah is given the nickname of the "Weeping
Prophet" (Jeremiah 9:1); however, there is so much more to Jeremiah's message
than just the tears he shed. He also shares the message that to be a follower of
God, we are often required to deliver unpopular messages at times when people
do not want to hear them, but it is precisely the messages that we need to hear
the most. We are often required, as followers of God, to deliver unpopular
messages when we feel utterly inadequate and powerless to do so, simply
because God tells us to share them.[60] This was Jeremiah's task in a time when
Judah was falling apart from the inside out, and perhaps it is our mission today
when our land appears to be heading down the same road. The only question
that should be asked of us … do we weep for our country or for our churches
as Jeremiah did for Judah? If not, why not?

I remember the time I was given no choice but to confront (and there
is no other word for what I had to do but confront) a pastor who was teaching
weak theology that had become false doctrine in the church he was leading. I
became physically ill over the issue. I put it off. Sadly, I avoided the
confrontation until the weak teaching had evolved into false doctrine, and it

---

[60] C. Hassell Bullock describes this sense of inadequacy so well when he
writes, "Jeremiah discharged his ministry with a peculiar yet creative fusion of
courage and reluctance." C. Hassell Bullock, *An Introduction to the Old Testament
Prophetic Books* (Chicago: Moody Books, 1986), 187. No wonder Jeremiah shed so
many tears, for anyone who illustrates this interpersonal struggle would have to
express his emotion in some way, and is there any better than tears?

was my sin for not addressing the issue earlier. Yes, it was my sin because I had procrastinated and allowed the pastor to "get away with" teaching bad theology. I had not been the Berean we are all commanded to be in Acts 17.

I would love to tell you that the pastor responded well to my efforts … but that would not be the case. It became ugly, even though I talked to the pastor privately, I was accused of trying to destroy what was being done at the church. I decided to leave the church quietly and without any fanfare. Still, the pastor made my leaving a public issue as he attempted to gather his supporters together in opposition to me. It was painful, but I would do it again … just a lot sooner. For delivering unpopular messages for a godly reason, as Jeremiah learned in his ministry, is one of the greatest spiritual battles we will ever face.

Jeremiah's Background and Time (1:1-3)

The son of Hilkiah, one of the priests in the city of Anathoth, was given the name Jeremiah ("may Jehovah lift up"). As one reads Jeremiah 1:1, it could be seen as nothing more than a standard biographical introduction to one of the Hebrew Scriptures (OT) books for a prophet. However, there is also a great deal of information given that could be overlooked by someone reading the book today if they are not paying attention. Anathoth was one of the Levitical cities established for the tribe of Benjamin as the Promised Land was being settled in the closing chapters of Joshua (21:17-18). Yet, there is a question related to Anathoth and Jeremiah's family lineage that is good for curiosity's sake, but is impossible to answer with any certainty, and it is related to what is found in 1 Kings 2:26-27.

In the 1 Kings passage, we see that Solomon banishes the High Priest, Abiathar, to Anathoth for his actions in 1 Kings 1:5-8 when the high priest sides with Adonijah in his rebellion against David. We also discover from the text that Abiathar was a descendant of Eli the prophet, who mentored Samuel. The only question that anyone is unable to answer with certainty is whether Jeremiah's family is a descendant of Abiathar … but the possibility definitely exists. If so, Jeremiah's lineage credentials would have been on a high pedestal as he began his prophetic ministry, perhaps one of the reasons he was fearful because he knew what it meant to cross a king. However, he also knew from his family lineage what it meant to follow the wrong path (i.e., Adonijah); therefore, he also knew he had no choice.

The "primary" kings of Judah during Jeremiah's prophetic ministry were Josiah, Eliakim/Jehoiakim, Jehoiachin (aka Jeconiah or Coniah), and

Zedekiah.[61] Josiah ruled from 640 to 609 BC/BCE, with Jehoiakim ruling from 609 to 598 BC/BCE, and Jehoiachin (a third son of Josiah) ruling for only three months in 598/597 BC/BCE. The final son of Josiah, Zedekiah, ruled for eleven years (597-586 BC/BCE) until Jerusalem was destroyed and the final citizens were dispersed to Babylon.[62] Of these kings, only Josiah was considered to be a good king in the sight of God, and it is only Josiah who is not mentioned as interacting negatively with Jeremiah.[63]

Jeremiah's Painful Calling (1:4-10)

There is a tendency by some in the Pro-Life movement to pull verses 4-5 out from the moorings of its context and show that Jeremiah, along with all humanity, was formed and known by God from before conception.[64] I should note that I am categorically Pro-Life as it relates to the abortion issue. I am one of those who does not make exceptions for rape, incest, or the life of the mother. However, one should not use Jeremiah 1:4-5 as a prooftext for your abortion position, for then you would be taking the verses out of context, even though God does know us before conception and we are a life from the moment we are conceived. Other verses in Scripture can better illustrate that life is always the correct choice in relation to the life of the pre-born. Let's not use Jeremiah's calling to make a Pro-Life argument.

Jeremiah's calling from God was specifically to him and for him – just as our calling and purpose are to us and for us. The use of the word "formed" in verse 5 had a profound impact on Jeremiah, as the analogy was repeated again in Jeremiah 18:1-11 and Lamentations 4:2. For this usage of "formed"

[61] 2 Kings 23-25 provides a summary overview of the kings during Jeremiah's ministry. I will not include Jehoahaz, the son of Josiah, in the description of a Judean king, as he ruled for only three months before being essentially kidnapped by the Pharaoh of Egypt, Neco II (23:30-33). Neco then installed Jehoahaz' brother Eliakim as the new king of Judah and changed his name to Jehoiakim. It should be noted that both kings were considered evil and committed evil acts in the sight of God (23:34-37).

[62] Bullock, *An Introduction to the Old Testament Books*, 192-95. See also entries on Jehoachin and Zedekiah in *Zondervan's Pictorial Bible Dictionary*, Merrill Tenney, gen. ed. (Grand Rapids: Zondervan, 1967), assorted pages for entries. Please note that I do not consider Gedaliah to be a rightful king of Judah, as he was a governor at the time he was appointed and was not a son of Josiah, and did not have a rightful claim to the throne, as he was the son of Shaphan and not in the lineage of David.

[63] Bullock, *An Introduction to the Old Testament Books*, 192-93.

[64] David Criswell, *Controversies in the Prophets: A Comparative Analysis of Controversies in the Hebrew Prophets* (North Charleston, SC: Fortress Adonai Press, 2007), 81-82.

was identifiable to the work of a potter who formed, shaped, destroyed, and recreated something beautiful through the work of his hands. Jeremiah was shaped/called by the Master Potter to be consecrated/set aside for a purpose – to be a prophet of God, not only to Judah but also to the nations of the world.

Jeremiah responded similarly as did the first leader of the Jewish people – Moses. Moses blamed his inability to speak well. Jeremiah used the excuse of his youthfulness. God did not allow Moses' speech impediment to be an excuse, and neither did he allow Jeremiah's age to be a justification for not obeying a call from God. Indeed, excuses never seem to go over well with God, for he sees beyond our frailties to see our abilities.

He told Samuel to look at the heart when he was inspecting the sons of Jesse. He told Eli not to throw Hannah out of the tabernacle when she was praying for a son just because he presumed she was drunk. He told Gideon to take a ridiculously small number of men against an army because he knew that "the battle belonged to the Lord" and 300 men were just enough. He saw Noah, and humanity was saved. I could go on and on, but I believe you are getting the message. Or at least I hope you are.

Yet, Jeremiah felt inadequate for the calling that God had on his life. I understand that feeling. I often ask God why he chose me to be a missionary, especially a missionary to the Jewish people. Surely … there must have been more qualified people than Amy Downey to be called. However, God chose me, and here I am, 25 years later, still seeking opportunities to share the Gospel message with the Jewish people. **Therefore, we should recognize that this calling of Jeremiah in the first chapter of his prophecy reflects a sense of personal inadequacy vs. God's overwhelming power.** The only question for us is whether we will allow the King of the universe to be sovereign in our lives, or do we prefer to wallow in our inadequate failings? Do we win or lose this spiritual warfare skirmish?

Additionally, and this is important as well, God responded to Jeremiah in much the same way as he did with another prophet of Jeremiah's time – Isaiah (Isaiah 6). God extended his power and caused Jeremiah's mouth to be touched with God's own words (v. 9). Yes, I recognize that I did not quote the verse as it is written in English, regardless of whatever translation someone might be reading from, and there is a reason for that fact. Why – our English words simply are too inadequate to describe what happened to Jeremiah in verse nine.

The Hebrew word that is translated as "hand" is the word "hand," but that is because how does anyone describe the immensity of God's actual power touching someone – and that is what happened. The word for "touched" is in the Hiphil Imperfect (see ***Missions in the Minor Key***, chapter 12 [p. 223ff.]

for a more detailed explanation of the Hiphil verb), which indicates that God himself caused Jeremiah's mouth to be touched. I don't know about you, but that must have been a static shock moment like no other! Isaiah experienced the seraphim placing coal on his tongue, but Jeremiah experienced God himself touching his mouth.

And what were the words that God gave to Jeremiah's mouth? Were they happy, cheerful words? Were they words of prosperity and wealth and hope? NOPE! They were brutal and uncomfortable words. They were painful words. They were words that no one would want to hear, much less share with the masses or the king. **This is because Jeremiah had to accept that his feelings of powerlessness were accurate but God's words are powerful and eternal.**

The word that is so often translated as "set over" can come across as bland and safe unless one looks deeper. The root word in Hebrew is *paqad,* and when it is in the Hiphil form (as it is here), it should be understood to mean that God was causing Jeremiah to be appointed as an overseer of over nations and kingdoms as God's prophet to root out, pull down, destroy, demolish, build, and plant. In other words, God was ensuring that Jeremiah would never win a popularity contest with the message he was ordained to share.

Being called to deliver a message that was guaranteed to be unpopular to a people who wanted to compromise spiritually, morally, and politically will not result in many invitations for dinner. Calling people to go against the tide when all people want to do is "Roll Tide" (sorry, University of Alabama fans, but the pun was just too obvious) will ensure that you will not be added to anyone's missionary support list. Asking people to change their ways when the winds of change are going in the opposite direction from God will often cause one to walk alone. Yet, this was Jeremiah's task, and anyone's responsibility who is willing to take up the armor of spiritual warfare. Why? Because sharing the hard message to hard people in hard times is never the definition of fun times, but it is a message they need to hear. Jeremiah knew this, and we need to learn it as well.

Now, let us consider the rest of Jeremiah's life before all of us (myself included) become too afraid to fight the rest of the battle that needs to be faced.

Questions for Individual or Group Study

1.   Without giving in to the tendency to give a "Sunday School Answer," what is your human response to the idea – **Spiritual warfare often requires us to deliver unpopular messages – especially when we feel inadequate and must lean on God's power to accomplish His work.**

2.   Have you ever been directed to share an unpopular message with someone and dreaded what the outcome might be? Did you do it or did you

find a way to avoid it? If you avoided it, what was the result of your avoidance? Was it negative for you or negative for the person who should have heard your message? Have you experienced guilt for not sharing the message?

3.   What is your excuse for not serving God when he calls you? A past sin, a present issue, a future fear? Do you think that your problem/issue/impediment is too large for God to get past? If God can use some of the sinful people in Scripture … why can he not use you for the calling he has on your life? Think about it…

4.   Are you prepared to recognize your powerlessness in the face of the enemy we face today? Yet … do we recognize the power of God's Words that we have been given to share? What is keeping any of us from fully utilizing the power of God's Word (Scripture) in our lives? What is the worst that can happen? What is the best that can happen? If the best/worst happens, what will change?

10

Spiritual Warfare Is Often About Appearing like a Complainer When You Are Just Grieving
(Jeremiah 4:19-31; 10:18-25; 12:1-17; 15:10-21; 20:7-18)

Spiritual warfare is about grieving the state of the world, for we can see the condition of the world and realize that while we might not be able to stop it, we can seek to slow it down.

When I was student teaching as the final component to complete my Bachelor of Science in Education (BSE) from East Texas Baptist University in the late 1990s (before the days of laptops and iPods), my supervising teacher was Anne Newman. She was one of those old-style teachers who ruled her classroom with fear and more than a bit of intimidation. However, she was an excellent teacher, and I am grateful that she was my supervisor.

As I was completing my student teaching days, Mrs. Newman told me she saw me as an idealist and was worried that I would get burned out with the desire to change the world. She had a point with her worry, but I assured her that I didn't want to change the world but only wanted to make a few dents in it. She looked at me quizzically over that remark, and for many years, I hung onto the card that Mrs. Newman gave me on my last day – a card showing a dented car on the front with her note to me on the inside that said, "I hope you make an impact on the world."

Anne Newman was not a Christian as far as I could ascertain, and so I do not know how she would feel about her idealistic student teacher becoming a missionary to the Jewish people. However, I think she would get a chuckle out of my continued efforts to make a few dents in the world as I seek to scatter Gospel seed to all the Jewish (and non-Jewish) people I meet, whether it is on planes or donut shoppes or wherever I might be. I also believe she might still worry about burnout for me, but just like Jeremiah, it is not physical exhaustion that breaks me down, but the spiritual condition of the world.

Therefore, this chapter will consider this aspect of Jeremiah's life and how his grief could have appeared, and indeed it sometimes was, as one who was deeply dissatisfied with the conditions of the world. Yet it was an expression of his heartbreak and longing for the people to return to God. A longing that would not happen, but a longing that Jeremiah still craved and sought from God. And while there are several passages listed in the chapter heading, we will primarily focus on 4:19-31, as this expresses the warrior's heartfelt anguish in language that we can all identify with at times in our own lives.

Laments Before the Book of Lamentations
(10:18-25; 12:1-17; 15:10-21; 20:7-18)

The book of Jeremiah expresses a series of laments (expressions of grief) from the prophet's mind and heart as Babylon approaches from the outside and the people of Judah begin to self-destruct from within. These emotional outbursts are from a human being who was overcome by what he was seeing and by the responsibility he had been given by God. C. Hassell Bullock describes it perfectly when he quotes the great Jewish scholar Abraham Joshua Heschel – "To be a prophet is both a distinction and an affliction."[65]

Jeremiah experienced this reality many times, and the passages noted in the heading of this chapter reflect this anguish and affliction. The Jeremiah 20:7-18 lament reflects a time after the prophet was placed in bonds by Pashur, the son of the priest Immer. In verse 7, Jeremiah cries out over a sense of being deceived by God since becoming God's spokesperson. He wanted to see those who had hurt him to be wounded (v. 12), and he lamented the day he had been born (v. 13-18). Yet even in all this expression of grief, Jeremiah still knew Jehovah was standing alongside him (v. 11), and so he knew he must continue the work he had been given by God … even though it brought pain.

And while on some level, and in the world today, this might be seen by some as almost an expression of Jeremiah being bipolar, it should not be. It is just Jeremiah expressing in far more eloquent language than what I wrote in my personal journal summary of this passage – "Spiritual warfare is sometimes an exercise of utter frustration, but I must remember that I have a calling to finish even if life sometimes stinks from time to time."

Yes, service to God does stink at times on a human level. Let's be honest about this truth. The truth that the wicked often do prosper is hard to endure during the best of times and impossible to face during the worst of times. I remember those times when I would vent to my mama about this reality, and she would say to me, "Amy, pray for the wicked, for they will either be judged in this world or the next. We must pray that they will be judged in this world because the judgment in the next world is eternal." This truth would humble me, but I would still fume because I felt as if the wicked were often not outside the church walls but within them.

Yes, I went there. I admit it, and so did Jeremiah in chapter 10 as he recounted God's righteous indignation over the actions of the priests (aka shepherds). Other versions translate their actions as stupid or dull-hearted, but the KJV uses the word "brutish," which I believe is the best word choice here.

---

[65] Bullock, *An Introduction to the Old Testament Prophetic Books*, 9, from Abraham J. Heschel, *The Prophets*, vol. 1 (New York: Harper & Row, 1962), 17-18.

The priests of Jeremiah's days had become so carnal and debased that they only cared for themselves, even while the sheep (the people of Judah) were spiritually and soon-to-be physically scattered, and the shepherds did not care (v. 21).

And while we must be careful not to be guilty of modern-day application of the texts in the Hebrew Scriptures, lest we become guilty of allegory, do we not see that to be true today as well in some places? Pastors and so-called Christian leaders who care more about their proximity to perceived power than the spiritual and moral needs of their people. Judah fell in Jeremiah's days because the Temple priests and the other prophets placated the sins of the powerful.

But for what reason … false and temporary power … what eternal good does that do anyone? It does not disciple the people. It does feed the spiritual needs of the people in the pews. It does not nurture those who are hurting. What eternal good does perceived power allocated from those who only want you for whatever you might provide to them give to anyone? The answer … NOTHING!

Jeremiah 10:18-25, especially the final verse of the chapter, tells us that even though he knew he stood alone against the tide, he knew he would also get swept up when the waves of judgment from God were cast down upon the people of Judah. Whew … tough reality for the righteous to face, but one that we might need to consider as well in this spiritual reality today. We will not be immune when God acts against hypocrisy in his house today. We must be prepared to stand strong when he does, because he will act because we have given him no choice.

Yes, I recognize there is no structure or organization to my laments in this section. I appear to go back and forth from one biblical passage to another. And I will admit that I am not going in chronological order, which is contrary to my perfectionistic pattern, because it represents not only Jeremiah's emotions but also, in many instances, our own. The downcast mood we experience in the morning from an annoying email can be overturned by an encouraging phone call from a friend in the afternoon. This does not make us necessarily mercurial or bipolar, but simply human. Jeremiah often went from one mood to another based on the circumstances of the spiritual battle he faced as a prophet, and so do we in the spiritual warfare circumstances we face, and no reality expresses this reality more clearly than the account we find in Jeremiah 12:1-17.

The first four verses of Jeremiah 12 express those very human emotions that can best be described by the three words of **"it's not fair."** We long for fairness in the world. We want the underdog to win and root against the supposed villain. We want the one who never should have had a chance to have a shot but to win against all odds. This was never more evident than on 16 March 2018 during what the college basketball world calls "March Madness."

The 16th-seeded Retrievers of the University of Maryland-Baltimore County (student enrollment of 13,906 in the fall of 2024) were playing the #1 seed University of Virginia Cavaliers (student enrollment of over 26,000 in 2024). The Virginia Cavaliers were not only the #1 seed in their region but were also considered the #1 team in the country. No one expected the Retrievers of UMBC to have a chance against the university founded by Thomas Jefferson in the 1700s. No one but the eleven men who played basketball for the Retrievers and their coach. This was the ultimate story of the underdog versus one of the big dogs of college basketball.

The game was tied at halftime, 21 to 21, but this was not unexpected. Virginia played a defensive game, and it was anticipated that they would bury UMBC after halftime. However, that was not what happened. The Retrievers instead buried the #1 team in the nation by scoring 54 points in the second half and won the game by twenty points. And … for the first time in the history of "March Madness" (which began in 1939), the 16th seed defeated the #1 seed and Cinderella lived to play another day.[66]

Isn't this what we all long for in our Christian life? That "one shining moment" when the spiritual villain is defeated here on earth, and we can understand why the pain and sorrows were worth all the work, discipline, and heartache?[67] But, and sadly, we, like Jeremiah, often are not given that moment or the video at the end of the tournament of life. In fact, God tells Jeremiah in verses 5-6 that his own family does not even have his back and are dealing treacherously against him. In other words, Jeremiah was not welcome at his own family reunion!

But … and before Jeremiah could feel too sorry for himself … God let him and us know that things could be worse. The focus of the remainder of

---

[66] Ryan Fagan, "History of 16 vs. 1 Upsets in March Madness: How Many 16 Seeds Have Won in NCAA Tournament?," *The Sporting News* (16 March 2025), available online at **https://www.sportingnews.com/us/ncaa-basketball/news/16-seed-1-upset-ncaa-tournament-umbc-virginia/1npv6h1jj87gy1jrl44jkndvzu**; accessed 22 April 2025.

[67] The phrase "one shining moment" is often associated with the NCAA College Basketball Tournament; therefore, it would be inappropriate not to give a source for the phrase. See, Paul M. Banks, "Exclusive: How Jim Nantz and Pat Sullivan Saved One Shining Moment," *The Sports Bank* (8 April 2025), available online at **https://www.thesportsbank.net/college-bball/north-carolina-tar-heels/jim-nantz-one-shining-moment-pat-sullivan/**; accessed 22 April 2025.

Jeremiah 12 is God expressing his own anguish to the prophet. God's broken heart as he sees his inheritance (aka heritage) taken into captivity due to the inadequacy of shepherds (leaders and priests) who failed his people (v. 7-10). God's broken heart as he becomes angry over the situation that the people have wrought upon themselves because of their own sinfulness and stupidity (v. 11-13). God's frustration is evident in these words in Jeremiah, and it is as if God is telling the prophet – "You are not the only one to feel this level of volatile emotions about all this is going on at the moment."

I don't know about you, but God's reaction to Jeremiah is somewhat comforting to me. The reality that God can become angry (albeit his anger is righteous indignation and mine rarely is) gives me both a sense of comfort and fear. Comfort because he sees what I see but fear because he will not tolerate our behavior forever. Yet, God is ever compassionate (v. 14-17) to those who do fear him and that is far more than we deserve and why his indignant anger is always righteous.

The final of these four laments that we need to briefly examine before getting to the core lament of this chapter (4:19-31) is from a time after God has informed Judah – even though they still do not wish to hear the bad news – that judgment is coming (15:10-21). And since Jeremiah is God's messenger, the reader can see in verse 10 that the prophet is unpopular with the people. He is a man of contention, and people are cursing him.

However, this reality of cursing him is not just hurling insults or bad words at him. The concept of a curse in Hebrew lore, and even in this grammatical form (Piel Participle – intensive and ongoing), lends itself to something that requires spiritual consideration. This idea is amplified when Rabbi Geoffrey Dennis writes, "In Jewish thought and texts, curses exemplify the belief that speech can have tremendous power."[68] In fact, the idea of "cursing" someone had become an amusing art form among Yiddish speakers in Eastern Europe in the late 19th and early 20th century. One such example is ***"Der Got vos hot geshpoltn dem yam vet dir shpaltn dem kop oykh!,"*** which can be translated as "The God who split the sea will split your head too!"[69] Yet, the idea of cursing someone was a powerful means of hurting

---

[68] Rabbi Geoffrey Dennis, "Jewish Curses: Magic and the Supernatural," My Jewish Learning, available online at **https://www.myjewishlearning.com/article/jewish-curses/**; accessed 23 April 2025.

[69] There is a plethora of examples that can be found on the internet. This particular example was found at **https://yiddishwit.com/gallery/split.html**; accessed 23 April 2025.

someone physically and spiritually, whether in a 19th-century European Shtetl or Jeremiah's day.

Indeed, words do hurt and the old adage about sticks/stones/words is nothing but a lie. Yet, the reality is that fighting the battle for God's cause is sometimes just being a "thorn in the flesh" to others because you are called to share an uncomfortable truth. Just like Jeremiah was called to do in his time. But … and Jeremiah had to learn this lesson as well … do not expect praise for the effort of being a truthteller – especially from your family (cf. 12:1-17).

Nope, it is not easy to be a truth teller, even if that is the primary action of being engaged in spiritual battle. Jeremiah vented (i.e., involved himself in unrighteous, self-serving indignation) in verses 14-18 and more times than we like to admit, so do we – or at least I will admit that I do. This does not mean that we have fallen in battle. It means we are human, but we must acknowledge that we have erred/sinned. And that is the message to Jeremiah in verses 19-21 – return and God will cause Jeremiah to be restored (Hiphil Imperfect).

Returning and returning and returning so that the good can be removed from the garbage – again a Hiphil Imperfect verb – is the action of a forgiving and restorative God who loves us despite our faults. This is why I have highlighted these last three verses in Jeremiah 15 in my Bible, for God is in the restoration business for his spiritual warriors, even though we fail and fail and fail again. He longs to make of us a strong wall of bronze that cannot be overcome even when the world fights against us.

But … we have to return and return and return to God. He will deliver us when we have lost the joy of our calling. He will redeem us when we have been sapped like a maple tree of the sweetness of our hope. However, we cannot find that restoration unless we return and return and return. Yes, I love these verses very much.

Heading Towards a Chaos of Our Own Making (4:19-31)

I separated this lament of Jeremiah's into its own section because, to be honest with you, this is where we are as churches and as a country (United States). We are heading towards a chaos of our own making. This might not be a popular view to write, but I believe it to be truthful and given the theme of this chapter, I have to say it do I not? For your information, I will go into more detail about this concept in the next chapter, but please read this section before skipping it and the next chapter.

The first part of Jeremiah 4 has already witnessed the prophecy that Judah will be invaded from the North (i.e., Babylon). This section (v. 19-31) is the response and is a heartbreaking lament and expression of anguish from what appears to be a variety of voices. As to the identity of all the voices, it is impossible to distinguish, but one can sense that at least two of the voices are

God and Jeremiah. Jeremiah's voice at the thought of the Temple being destroyed and God's heartbreak over punishing his Chosen children … even though it was earned and justified.

In verses 19-22, one can read about a contrast in reactions between what God/Jeremiah sees coming and how the people respond to the reality that Babylon is approaching. This contradiction is summarized in verse 22 when God apparently calls the people foolish and silly (NAS – stupid; KJV – sottish). Now I have to admit that the word "sottish" was a word that I had to look up to glean the whole meaning, but when I did, I enjoyed the definition and appreciated the KJV's interpretation. The online source "The Free Dictionary" defines it as "stupefied from or as if from drink."[70]

Therefore, one gets the sense from the KJV that the people were so drunk on their pride and presumption about their status with God that they thought they were untouchable. They had become, as verse 22 states, "they are wise to do evil, but to do good they have no knowledge." The tenses for the words are the Hiphil Infinitive, which shows that they had "cause to do good," but they chose to "have cause to do evil." In other words, they knew better but didn't care.

I believe the argument could be made that Christians today are in the same boat as Jeremiah's people. We as a collective are too foolish to realize that we are heading towards chaos, yet we cheer on events that will lead to our own destruction. We in America seem to believe we are protected from evil because we are Christians, yet ignore the martyrdom of our brothers and sisters around the world who are guilty of so much less than we are. We as American churches are foolish enough to believe that if we just elect the "right people," everything will be calm and secure – even though that has never been successful in Christian history.

Verses 23-26 provide an analogy/metaphor that should remind people of what could be called a reverse of the creation narrative found in Genesis 1. This description, which should not be overlooked in our rush to move on to happier thoughts in verses 27-31, helps us see that we are heading toward a madness of our own making. Destruction and turmoil are the opposite of creation, and Judah (we) was/are the cause of it all.

However, verses 27-31 offer hope that Judah did not deserve it, but God is merciful. This absence of **a complete** destruction is because of God's promises and not because of anything good that Judah might have done. This

---

[70] *American Heritage Dictionary of the English Language*, 5th ed. (NY: Houghton Mifflin Harcourt Publishing, 2016); available online at **https://www.thefreedictionary.com/sottish**; accessed 30 April 2025.

is the same promise that Jesus gave to the disciples in Matthew 16:17-19 when he told them all (not just Peter) that the gates of hell would not prevail against his church. For while there are times it might appear dark with the winnowing of the harvest time, God will deliver his people through the threshing floor.

So … what does this passage from Jeremiah have to do with spiritual warfare? It is the reality that sometimes seeing destruction and realizing that it cannot be stopped is one of the most difficult aspects of a Christian's life. Fighting what appears to be a losing battle against the spiritual forces that come from within and without churches can be beyond spiritually debilitating. It can be backbreaking and soul-crushing.

I saw my daddy die from what I would describe as spiritual knife wounds in the back that were delivered at the hands of people who called him a friend one day and ignored him the next. Missionaries and pastors are struggling with burnout at a rate that would shock the average churchgoer. Yet, and while many individuals in ministry do burn and flame out, one of the greatest acts of discipleship is to seek to make those infamous dents in the world and to seek to slow down what might appear to be inevitable. For if we can do battle on behalf of one soul, then the struggle is eternally worth it.

Questions for Individual or Group Study

1.   Without giving in to the tendency to give a "Sunday School Answer," what is your human response to the idea – **Spiritual warfare is about grieving the state of the world, for we can see the condition of the world and realize that while we might not be able to stop it, we can seek to slow it down.**

2.   What is your response to the following quote from Abraham Joshua Heschel – "To be a prophet is both a distinction and an affliction?" Do you agree with the point that Heschel is making, or do you see it as an affront to the call that a prophet is given? Based on your response to the above question, do you see spiritual warfare as a blessing or as an affliction, and why?

3.   No one likes to be disliked. No one likes to be hated. However, Jesus told the disciples shortly before he went to the Garden of Gethsemane that the world would hate them because the world hates him (John 15). Why should we expect anything different today? Given this truth, how do you respond to the idea that we will be despised/hated for taking a stand for our Christian values, our moral values? Do you find yourself keeping your views private so as not to draw attention to your Christian position? Are you silent so as not to be offensive? Why or why not? Is there a way to be truthful in today's world while also not being angry? How do you walk the tightrope?

4.   Do you believe that the spiritual battle you are facing is worth it, even if one life can be changed because you did not quit? Why or Why not? If you

answered yes to the question, why do you believe so many Christians quit the struggle and either become apathetic to the Christian battles we are called to fight or turn away from the warfare altogether? If you answered no to the question, why do you feel that one soul that could be changed is not worth it?

11

Spiritual Warfare Is Often About Standing up
When No One Else Will
(Jeremiah 7:1-11; 26:1-15)

Spiritual warfare is often about declaring an unpopular, uncomfortable message that will not be received well, but it requires finding the courage to do so anyway.

Most people, even those within the inner sanctums of the Southern Baptist Convention (i.e., Nashville), have never heard of the Southern Baptist missionary Jacob Gartenhaus. And why would they? There is no building at any seminary named after Dr. Gartenhaus, and there is no mission offering named after this missionary, who served faithfully with the Home Mission Board (now known as NAMB) for almost thirty years. He served faithfully during the darkest days of the Great Depression, I might add.

So ... just who was Jacob Gartenhaus?[71] He was a Jewish believer in Jesus who was born in 1896 in what was then the Austria-Hungary Empire but is now Poland. He was raised as an Orthodox Jewish man who longed to see the world, especially after a childhood illness that opened his eyes to the fact that there was more to life beyond his shtetl (village) in Eastern Europe. He arrived in America in 1915 and was led to believe in Jesus as Messiah by his brother, who had also become a believer after leaving home.

Gartenhaus received his training at Moody Bible Institute and The Southern Baptist Theological Seminary, and in 1921 was hired by the Home Mission Board (HMB) as the first missionary to the Jewish people in North

---

[71] I gave a paper/presentation at the Evangelical Theological Society on the mission life of Jacob Gartenhaus during his years with the Southern Baptist Convention -- "The Misunderstood Life, Mission, and Ministry of Jacob Gartenhaus - Or How to 'Be Cancelled' by Southern Baptists in the 1940s," November 2023, San Antonio, Texas. For additional information on the life of Jacob Gartenhaus, I would encourage you to read his autobiography, *Traitor?: A Jew, A Book, A Miracle* (Nashville: Thomas Nelson, 1980), primarily pages 1-100.

America.[72] Dr. Gartenhaus served until 1949, when he was forced to retire from the HMB due to an accusation of what we would today call sexual harassment of a fellow missionary – Lucille McKinney.[73]

And while that would and could be the end of the story for Jacob Gartenhaus and his work as a missionary, there is more to the story. And the reason I am sharing his story as an introduction to this chapter (for I have no use for someone who harasses or abuses anyone – whether they be male or female).

In November 1952, Lucille McKinney wrote a letter to the executive committee of the HMB retracting her accusation with the following statement: "forgiveness is asked for having wronged an innocent man."[74] The HMB determined that a retraction of the accusation made against Gartenhaus should be made public, and it was, but on page nine of the April 1953 issue of *Southern Baptist Home Missions*.

And while I admit that this is mere theory, I do believe I know why Jacob Gartenhaus was "targeted" for lack of a better word for his firing by the Southern Baptist Convention and the Home Mission Board. It all began in 1934 when he spoke the truth about Adolf Hitler and the Third Reich's plans for the destruction of the Jews during the Baptist World Alliance meeting in Berlin, Germany.

The Baptist World Alliance remains, to this day, a gathering of Baptists from around the world and diverse evangelical perspectives, who gather every four years to discuss areas of commonality and difference. In 1934, they gathered in Berlin even though Adolf Hitler and the Nazi Party had come to

---

[72] Gartenhaus was approved as an HMB missionary due to a 1875 SBC resolution developed by Dr. Crawford Toy that was approved by the convention. There are two interesting aspects to this resolution, (1) it sadly took forty-six years from the passing of the resolution to hire a missionary to reach the Jewish people and (2) Crawford Toy was almost the husband of renowned husband of famed SBC missionary Lottie Moon who turned down his proposal to go to China until she died in 1912.

[73] Minutes of the Executive Committee of the Home Mission Board [HMB] – 3 March 1949. An article announcing his "retirement" can be found in the *Southern Baptist Home Missions* (April 1949).

[74] Minutes of the Executive Committee of the Home Mission Board (HMB) – November 1952. It should be noted that during my research for the ETS presentation, I visited the official SBC library in Nashville. While I found extensive notes on the mission life of Jacob Gartenhaus, I was unable to locate either the original accusatory letter or the retraction.

power in January 1933, and one could argue it should have been moved to a different location.

Jacob Gartenhaus went to Berlin to collect information about the troublesome rumors coming from Germany – rumors about the attacks on German Jews, regardless of their belief or non-belief in Jesus. Other SBC leaders, including M. E. Dodd and Ben Bridges, went to Germany to attend the meeting. However, their reactions to the Third Reich Germany that they saw were vastly different from that of Gartenhaus, and one could surmise that this is when Gartenhaus' troubles began.

Jacob Gartenhaus wrote upon his return from the BWA meeting for *The Atlanta Constitution* (3 September 1934) that German Jews were being "murdered every day in Germany" and that German Jewish believers had left their homeland "not because they were Baptists but because Jewish blood coursed through their veins." However, Ben Bridges who was the General Secretary for the Arkansas Southern Baptists reported even before going to the BWA Berlin meeting such ideas that perhaps "Herr Hitler might be 99 44/100% right in his activity and attitude toward the Jews in Germany" and that maybe Hitler was right in wishing "to purge itself of such foreigners."[75] M. E. Dodd, who was the president of the SBC Convention at the time and is to this day considered the founder of the Cooperative Program (the method by which SBC churches give to missions), wrote of his BWA observations the following:

> On this point it was revealed from many sources that the recent movements in Germany against the Jewish were not religious or racial but political and economic… Naturally excesses occurred and irresponsible persons committed some atrocious deeds. But at the worst it was not one-tenth as bad as we had been made to believe.[76]

Gartenhaus spoke out against the president of the SBC Convention and the leader of the SBCs in Arkansas. He spoke out against Nazi atrocities, not in a SBC publication but in a secular newspaper – and one of the largest newspapers in the South. Gartenhaus spoke out, and he continued to do so from that moment forward in every convention report he submitted about

---

[75] Ben Bridges, "Baptist, Hitler, and the Jews," *Arkansas Baptist* (29 March 1934), page 16.

[76] M. E. Dodd, "My Impressions of the Baptist World Congress," *Baptist and Reflector* (13 September 1934), page 5.

what was happening in Europe.[77] He became a thorn in the SBC's flesh, and ultimately, the flesh eliminated the thorn in 1949 with a false complaint against Jacob Gartenhaus.

I recognize that this introduction to the chapter has been rather lengthy, and I want to assure you, as the reader, that Dr. Gartenhaus continued his work as a missionary to the Jewish people until he died in 1984 in Chattanooga, Tennessee. He founded the mission organization International Board of Jewish Missions, which remains a Jewish evangelistic mission to this day.

However, I believe what happened to Jacob Gartenhaus serves as a good starting point for this chapter. For like Jeremiah, Gartenhaus delivered a message that was uncomfortable and awkward for the hearers, yet still he delivered it. He delivered it because it needed to be heard. And today, there are messages which need to be proclaimed even when the hearers (those within our own enclaves) will resist the message – sometimes very strongly. Jeremiah was persecuted. Gartenhaus was persecuted. Are we willing to be persecuted … even by those we believe to be friends?

Two Awkward Sermons – One Uncomfortable Truth (7:1-11; 26:1-15)

I remember being young and standing alongside my daddy at the church's front door as the service ended one Sunday morning. The church members were saying their goodbyes and repeating the typical phrase, "Good sermon, pastor," as they walked out the door. However, one deacon's wife looked even more peeved than her usual cranky self, looked at daddy and said, "You really stepped on my toes this morning, Brother Jack."

I believe she thought daddy would apologize for his sermon; however, I do not believe she could have anticipated my daddy's not-so-contrite response. Daddy looked her straight in the eye and, without skipping a beat, said, "I'm sorry, Sister Pruitt, I didn't mean to step on your toes. I was aiming for your heart."

As you can imagine, Sister Pruitt was not pleased with daddy's response, and I am sure that Sunday lunch included roast pastor with the fried chicken and mashed potatoes that were warming on her stove. And just like daddy's sermon many years ago, these two sermons of Jeremiah from chapters 7 and 26 were not aimed at the listener's toes but at the heart of the people in

---

[77] I reviewed all of Jacob Gartenhaus' SBC Convention reports from 1921 to 1948 for my ETS presentation – and there were many reports! However, I will not include any of those reports in this introduction. However, his reports during the World War II years are a heartbreaking read if you ever choose to examine them for yourself.

attendance. Both of Jeremiah's sermons were delivered at the gate of the Temple (Lord's House). However, the second was meant specifically to be heard by the priests and prophets who labored in the Temple, because while all of Judah was guilty, it was specifically the spiritual leaders who were found wanting in the eyes of God.

In both sermons (ch. 7 and 26), God commands Jeremiah to "Stand in the gate/court of the Lord's house..." The purpose of this placement was to be the exact opposite of the Walmart greeter – Jeremiah's job was to get in the way of the people entering and leaving the Temple and announce judgment UNLESS there was repentance in the land.

The phrase in 7:3 is to "amend your ways and deeds/doings;" however, the Hebrew for ways is the word *derekh,* which is the idea of path. Therefore, we should understand that Jeremiah is communicating to the people that it is time to return to the right road/path, for they are going in the wrong direction. This was an important message and a connecting point to verse 4 because the people in Jeremiah's days were assuming that just because they were the Chosen People … they could do as they wanted and worship as they willed, and they would be protected.

Jeremiah had to deliver a harsh message in verses 5-11, a message that their assumptions were way off, and that judgment was coming. A message that was continued in verses 12 and following (i.e., what happened to the Northern Kingdom is evident that God's patience will only last so long). The people had to begin practicing justice within the community, had to learn not to oppress (exploit) the strangers, the orphans, the widows, had not to shed innocent blood, and ultimately not follow other gods (v. 4-6, 9, 11). Then and only then will God deliver them and allow them to be delivered from the Babylonians, who are coming.

Definitely, not a fun message to deliver at the gate/court of the Temple, and one can assume that he preached some semblance of the same message in chapter 26. The people (especially the priests and prophets in ch. 26) were not fond of this message and wanted to sentence Jeremiah to death (26:11). So … did this cause Jeremiah to shrink from the message that God called him to deliver? Absolutely not! Instead, we see Jeremiah in 26:14-15 rise to the occasion with words that we should all take to heart and memory: ***"As for me, behold, I am in your hand: do with me as seemeth good and meet unto you. But know ye for certain, that if ye put me to death, ye shall surely bring innocent blood upon yourselves, and upon this city, and upon the inhabitants thereof: for of a truth the Lord hath sent me unto you to speak all these words in your ears."***

I will admit that these are tough words from Jeremiah, both the sermon and the warning in chapter 26, but they were and are necessary words today.

Words that need to be heard and delivered by people brave enough to say them. People who are brave enough to aim for the heart and not just the toes. People who are willing to stand up to the "Father of the Cooperative Program" and say that Hitler is a monster … not just the country's leader.

What you are reading in this chapter and what I am writing is perhaps today's greatest act of spiritual warfare that needs to be fought. We live in a world today where there are too many people within the church who ignore the sins of the church. Jeremiah did not overlook the sins of the people of his day. The prophets Micah, Joel, Amos, Obadiah, Nahum, Hosea, and others did not overlook the sins of the people. Jesus overturned the tables within the Temple courtyard. Paul called out the sins of the church of Corinth. So must we … even if it makes us the unpopular one because we are delivering an uncomfortable message.

Being the warrior that we are called to be requires us to deliver truth in the darkness. Fighting spiritual warfare begins in the house of God more often than anywhere else. Be a Jeremiah even if Sister Pruitt roasts you over her fried chicken and mashed potatoes. Be a Jeremiah even if lies are spread about you, like they were about Jacob Gartenhaus, because eventually, truth wins out. Be a spiritual warrior because God called you to be one.

"As for me, behold, I am in your hand: do with me as seemeth good and meet unto you. But know ye for certain, that if ye put me to death, ye shall surely bring innocent blood upon yourselves, and upon this city, and upon the inhabitants thereof: for of a truth the Lord hath sent me unto you to speak all these words in your ears." – Jeremiah 26:14-15

Questions for Individual or Group Study

1.   Without giving in to the tendency to give a "Sunday School Answer," what is your human response to the idea – **Spiritual warfare is often about declaring an unpopular, uncomfortable message that will not be received well, but finding the courage to do so anyway.**

2.   What is your response to the lengthy introduction account of what happened to Jacob Gartenhaus? Would you have stood up beside Dr. Gartenhaus in 1934? Given that he was proven innocent of the sexual harassment charges, what do you think should be done by the SBC today to restore his reputation?

3.   Could you follow God's leading to deliver a sermon like Jeremiah did in chapter 7? Does Jeremiah 26:14-15 frighten you, especially in light of the call for a death sentence from the priests and prophets? What would your response be?

12

Spiritual Warfare Is Often About Giving up Those Human Dreams for God's Ultimate Calling (Jeremiah 16:1-13)

Spiritual warfare is knowing that the dreams will still come, but knowing that they will never be fulfilled/realized because God's visions for you are greater than anything you could have imagined for yourself.

I wrote about "Scott" in chapter two, and so I won't repeat the story of the one who "got away" again. And while the loss of my dream of marrying Scott and having his children still can cause a pang in my heart, and I still have moments when I want to cry at the lost dream, even thirty years later. The reality is that not having a wedding ring on my hand or hearing someone call me mama is not the only loss someone can experience in life.

I have seen friends go through divorces so painful that I believe death would have been easier for them. I have seen people lose a child, and I would not wish that loss on anyone – even someone who has hurt me to the core of my being. The grief of that moment is beyond measure and lives with one forever. Truly … personal loss is one of those undefinable words that cannot be measured on a football field or in a sporting event. Personal loss takes a piece of one's soul and leaves behind a vacuum that can never truly be filled again.

So … how can I write the thesis sentence that I wrote above – **spiritual warfare is knowing that the dreams will still come, but knowing that they will never be fulfilled/realized because God's visions for you are greater than anything you could have imagined for yourself.** This is because the dreams will still come. I still have those longings for marriage, even though the reality of motherhood has long passed me by because of age and the reality that my name is not Sarah. My friends who went through a horrible divorce still wish it had not happened. I have no doubt my cousins who lost their child to suicide longed for the chance they could have stopped him from making that decision. Yet, and this includes my cousins who never stopped grieving for their sweet son, know that God's visions for our lives are far greater than anything that we could have envisioned for ourselves. This is why Jeremiah could write a verse that is so often taken out of context, in 29:11, "For

I know the thoughts that I think toward you, saith the Lord, thoughts of peace, and not of evil, to give you an expected end."[78]

The Loss of Jeremiah's Dream ... the Rise of God's Plans (16:1-13)

When God told me that singleness was my destiny in life (read chapter two again), it was not something I saw as a gift for my life. Yes, I know what Paul wrote in 1 Corinthians 7, but for me, it was a struggle, not something I wanted or desired for my life. However, I also know that my life would look completely different if I had married Scott and had the four children I envisioned all those years ago.

I would not have become the missionary I was called to become when I was sixteen years ago. I would not have traveled to twelve countries and shared the mission of Jewish evangelism on four continents. I would not have met so many amazing people, including seven Holocaust survivors. So ... it was a gift in many ways, but one that does not fill those lonely nights or ease the ache on those days when I see friends on Facebook celebrating anniversaries or showing pictures of their children and now their grandchildren. Singleness, while perhaps a gift from God I was given, was still the loss of a dream that still hurts at the most unexpected of times.

Therefore, I have always identified with the first two verses of Jeremiah 16 and perhaps even read too much into what was said to Jeremiah. However, and pleading my case, how could one not? God tells us it is not good for man to be alone (Gen. 2:18). Marriage was the first union in Scripture. The family is the standard by which all other designs are to be measured in creation.

Additionally, I can only find two examples in the Bible where someone is given a specific mandate regarding their marital status, and neither has a positive outcome. Hosea is told to marry the prostitute Gomer. Jeremiah is told to remain single. Yet, the death of a human dream, as Jeremiah had to have discovered (and I imagine Hosea as well), was to illustrate a message to the people that God knew would gain their attention. And sometimes, we will be asked to deny our own dreams for God's greater purpose as well. This is also a measure of spiritual warfare that is infinitely hard to respond to God in the

---

[78] Why do I believe this verse is taken out of context by so many? Because we need to look at the context of the passage – Jeremiah was writing to people who were already in captivity in Babylon. He was writing to those whose dreams had already been shattered, and Jeremiah was telling them to build a life where they are and trust in God's plans for them, and not to follow the words of false prophets. In other words, Jeremiah was telling them that while dreams still come ... God's plans are greater than anything they could have ever envisioned for their lives.

affirmative; yet, it is one that must be given over to God for his purposes to be achieved.

So what was God's purpose in requiring this of Jeremiah, and what can we as warriors who are struggling through the sludge of spiritual warfare today in the 21st century learn? God tells Jeremiah in verses 3-4 that the children, mothers, and fathers of Judah will soon be dead. However, this death will be horrific, and their bodies will be left out on the ground to rot and to become food for the birds and the scavengers of the earth.

What a prophetic message for Jeremiah to hear from God. It was a message of utter devastation and loss, a message of no hope and a vision that surely must have scarred the prophet. However, God's words were only going to grow worse. Verses 5-8 instructed Jeremiah not to grieve with the people and not to offer comforting words to those who were hurting.

Imagine a prophet or a minister of God who is told not to offer any words of comfort to someone who has reached the lowest moment, but must have been seeking hope. But … Jeremiah is denied the right to comfort his people by the God of the Jewish people. How difficult. How hopeless that must have been for both Jeremiah and the people who were swamped by grief and loss. However, Jeremiah could not offer comfort, for the truth was that it would have been false hope and a lie.

To sit **shiva** (the Jewish ritual of mourning over the dead) as described in verses 6-8 would have been a false front for Jeremiah, and that is not real consolation. Telling the truth is the only form of genuine consolation – even if the truth hurts. And to be honest with you, that is why I hate the Christian clichés that we have become so fond of spouting. Sometimes it is not going to get better, and it is not darkest just before the dawn, and your grandmother is not in a better place now that she is dead. The Christian cliches (aka lies) that we love to share because the truth is awkward, uncomfortable, or painful need to give way to the awkward, uncomfortable, and painful reality. For there are times when the grandmother does go to hell, and life is not going to get any better than it is right now.

My dad often pulled out a funeral sermon that was compassionate yet honest if the person he was "preaching over" was most likely or certainly feeling the fires of hell, while people were crying over his body/ashes. It was the story of the Rich Man and Lazarus from Luke 16:19-31. Daddy's approach was to compare the lives of the two men who both died and to focus on what the Rich Man would do if he could only return and tell his family the truth. Daddy did not tell them their loved one was in hell (unless the family asked for the truth to be spoken aloud), but he did not promise them that their family member was in Heaven either. He simply offered them the way to go to Heaven and to avoid the torments of hell. Everyone knew the not-so-subtle implication that my daddy was offering to the family, but no one could deny the truth either.

For truth matters today … now more than ever. And while people might follow in the same path as they did in Jeremiah's days (v. 10-13), and question and deny any fault for their situation and/or God's judgment. We are called to stand strong and proclaim the truth of God regardless of how they respond. God's truth, therefore, often requires us to make personal sacrifice, often requires us to allow personal dreams to die, and often requires us to let go of what was once so vitally important to us.

For Jeremiah, it was perhaps a wife and children. For me, it was being married to "Scott" and having a comfortable life in suburbia with his four children (FYI – I can still tell you the names of the children I never birthed). And even though it has been almost thirty years since I have had any contact with Scott, there is a part of me that wonders "what if" from time to time. Yet, the death of that particular dream has given way to plans and dreams from God that were beyond anything that I could have asked or imagined.

Opportunities to meet extraordinary people who have touched and even broken my heart, due to the fact that some of them rejected the truth of Messiah Jesus before they died, but people I treasure in my heart and soul. And while nice Christians have reprimanded me for saying that Josef and others are in hell because they rejected Jesus as Messiah, I say this truth because it is true, and it needs to be spoken today more than ever. I find only heartbreak in this truth, and I grieved alone when Josef died, but I follow the mandates of God rather than the whims of man.

Yes, human dreams often die when one decides to take up the warfare cross of Jesus, but the battle is calling, and the warriors are not as many as you might imagine. Are you willing to fight for him today … or not?

Questions for Individual or Group Study

1.   Without giving in to the tendency to give a "Sunday School Answer," what is your human response to the idea – **Spiritual warfare is knowing that the dreams will still come, but knowing that they will never be fulfilled/realized because God's visions for you are greater than anything you could have imagined for yourself.**

2.   Imagine if you were Jeremiah and told by God not to grieve with the people in their time of loss – due to the fact that God was judging them for their sins. What is your response to God? What is your response to the people? Can you reconcile what God is asking you to do in light of your innate personality and the giftedness that has been given to you by God? What do you do and how do you do it?

3.   Does truth matter today now more than ever? Can you define truth in an objective way without being guilty of defining it subjectively so that no one becomes angry with you? Why is it so hard to be Godly truthful today?

13

Spiritual Warfare Is Often About Hitting
Rock Bottom and Believing Anyway
(Jeremiah 38:1-13)

Spiritual warfare is about never changing God's message even after experiencing your own personal "well experience" … sometimes even from your own friends, family, and people closest to you.

The time was the summer of 1973. I was going to turn four years old in September, and my life was fairly normal by the world's standards. Mama was a housewife. My sister had been the smartest student in her class. Daddy worked for El Paso Natural Gas in the Four Corners region of New Mexico, where I had been born. Life was good for the three-year-old Amy.

Amy at Four Years Old

We went to church every Sunday. My parents worked in the children's church area where they served not only the church kids of First Baptist Church, Bloomfield, but also the Navajo children who were picked up from the reservation every Sunday on the bus. Everything about our lives looked normal. And it was only mama who knew that daddy was hiding a secret that was tearing him apart spiritually.

In 1963, two years after their marriage, daddy had surrendered to Christian ministry. He even went as far as looking at a small Christian college in East Texas – ironically the one I was working at when I finally surrendered to my mission call. He was unable to find a job or housing for them, and so he walked away from the call … in 1963.

Ten years later, along with two kids under the age of ten, the calling from God had never left him. It had only grown larger and louder in his mind and heart. He was struggling, and then suddenly, mama became ill with a severe case of E. coli and spent several days in the hospital. Even as a child of three, I remember daddy picking up mama from the hospital and picking up bits and pieces of their conversation from the front seat. Words like "is this a warning" and "it is my fault" came from daddy's mouth, and then, what seemed like only a few days later, we were packing boxes, cleaning out the house, and moving to Louisville, Kentucky.

Daddy had already been praying about this small Bible college in Louisville, and mama's illness apparently was the push he needed to commit to enter Christian service. The church in Bloomfield, NM, sent us off with an overflowing "Money Tree" and many verses of "I Have Decided to Follow Jesus." The Downey Family was headed to Kentucky, but first, we had to stop in West Texas to say goodbye to my grandparents.

I am not certain which set of grandparents was most opposed to this move to Kentucky. Daddy's side, especially Gramma, who was concerned about never seeing their grandchildren again. Mama's mother was worried about the financial issues that lay before us and whether or not we would be asking for money from them. What I do remember, however, as I sat beside daddy in the moving van while mama and my sister were in the car behind us as we drove away into the great unknown, was that I was looking through the side mirror of the van and seeing my grandparents just shaking their heads in confusion and perhaps even a little disappointment.

Four days later, we arrived in Louisville, but not before Daddy's pickup, which was being towed by the moving van, had four flat tires. We arrived in Louisville during the middle of the OPEC gas embargo when gas skyrocketed from $0.25 to $0.75 a gallon – the good old days! We also arrived in Louisville with no place to live and no job for daddy.

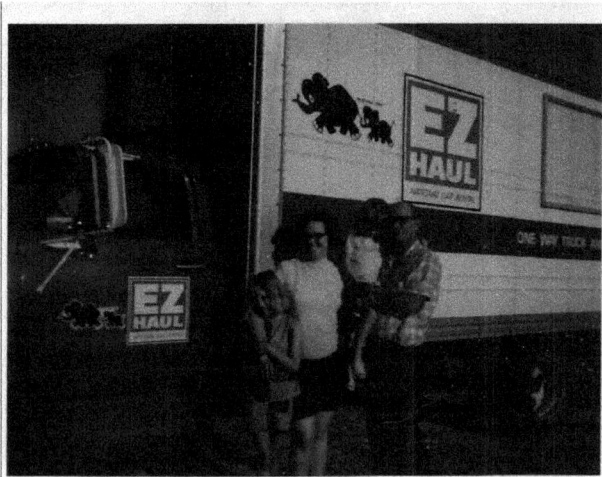

Moving to Kentucky

A place to live was found within a day. Mama began to babysit the children of professors at the school. Daddy, who had a fear of hospitals, which is not a good thing for people in ministry, could only find a position as the custodian at the Baptist Hospital in Louisville. And … we stayed in Louisville until daddy graduated from Bible college because Luke 9:62 was embedded in our family's hearts.

Was it easy? Absolutely not. The weekly grocery budget for our family of four was ridiculously low … yet we always had food on the table. We experienced a Salvation Army Christmas because my parents loved us enough to swallow their pride so my sister and I could have Christmas presents. A devastating tornado hit Louisville in April 1974, and we were cut off from communicating with our family back in Texas for almost a week as telephones were still connected to the walls of the house with cords. However, we were happy and we were in God's perfect will as a family.

The rest of my daddy's ministry life was not easy either; however, Jack and Barbara Downey were united against all spiritual and personal foes that stood against them. Sometimes, even when the opposition came from their own parents. Daddy and mama experienced those deep well moments as Jeremiah did in chapter 38, but they stood strong because they were together in the work of the Gospel. This truth was the only thing that made the work bearable and possible until daddy heard the call to go home to Heaven on July 4, 2000.

Jeremiah was not as fortunate as Jack Downey. He did not have a Barbara standing beside him during the lonely days of service to God … especially while sitting and/or standing at the bottom of a well. Yet, the prophet found the will to go on even while in the literal muck and mire, and thankfully, he did discover the man Ebed-Melech.

Sharing the Truth – Being Tossed into a Well (38:1-13)

The entirety of Jeremiah 38 presents a fascinating account of Jeremiah's obedience, the testimony of Ebed-Melech (whom we will discuss further in this chapter), and the ambivalent kingship of Zedekiah. Unfortunately, we do not have the space to discuss verses 14-28 except in a brief sentence or two. However, I would encourage you to continue reading to the end of the chapter and beyond to discover what happens when a king like Zedekiah waffles in his decision-making – especially when his country depends on good leadership.

Chapter 38 opens with four men hearing the warning of God, as conveyed through Jeremiah, about what was to come to the land through Nebuchadnezzar and Babylon. Instead of seeking God's forgiveness, these four men – Shephatiah, Gedaliah, Jucal, and Pashur – run (v. 1-4) to the king to tell him what was being said and to ask for Jeremiah's death because he was weakening the resolve of the people to fight what was coming.

And, indeed, Jeremiah was pronouncing judgment on the city and the land. He was telling the people that Judah would fall to Babylon. The accusation was not false; however, the rationale and/or motive behind their desire for Jeremiah's death was far from pure and holy. These four men were the princes of Jerusalem, and at least two of them were priests in the Temple. Jeremiah's words were a threat to their access to power that they had with Zedekiah. And if Judah did fall, their power would fall as well. They could not risk King Zedekiah taking advice from Jeremiah – for it would cause their influence to wane and their power to be no more.

By the way, did you count how many times I used the word "power" in the last two sentences? It was three times, for while the love of money is the root of all evil, the promise of power and influence, I would argue, is the essence of the first sin in the Garden of Eden. For money is fickle, it will appear one day and vanish the next, but power is the aphrodisiac that lingers forever. People murder for power. Wars are fought for power. Power brings money and fame and destruction. And that is why the four princes of Judah longed for Jeremiah to be silenced forever because they believed he would be a detriment to their power, never realizing that their perceived influence was nothing but a sham that would soon end.

We live in such a world today. We also live in such a church society today. People seemingly do not want to listen to the wisdom that comes from Scriptures, but the advice that is given from television "life coaches" disguised as megachurch pastors who hold up a Bible but never actually utilize its words in a sermon. But … somehow their words have more influence than their local church pastor because they have access to the White House. Yet, we never ask what biblical truth they had to give up to be granted entry to the Oval Office. Perhaps it is time we did and forsake the modern-day individuals who are not named Shephatiah, Gedaliah, Jucal, and Pashur, but ones that regularly show up on the Christian television station that needs to be avoided as well.

Zedekiah caved to the pressure of these four men and allowed Jeremiah to be thrown into the cistern, the well, of his son Malchiah (father of Pashur). This well/cistern has no water in it, but it is described as being muddy ("mire" in the KJV). One would expect that even a dry well would have mud at the bottom, but there is more to this description of "mire" than just a mixture of water and dirt for Jeremiah. It was a symbolic representation of Jeremiah hitting rock bottom.

Hitting rock bottom emotionally, personally, and spiritually is something that can destroy a person. Perhaps you have been there. I know I have been there (more than once) and I felt as if the wind had been sucked out of me and replaced by nothing. I was gasping for air and finding nothing to inhale. I was scrambling around looking for hope and only found more hopeless realities. This was Jeremiah at the bottom of the cistern,[79] and if one is engaged in the reality of spiritual warfare ... you will find yourself trapped in muck and mire more often than on top of the mountain. Are you encouraged yet?

Yet, and when Jeremiah must have been at his lowest, the king's servant literally for that is what his name means, Ebed-Melech (servant of the king), came to Jeremiah's rescue. There are several interesting aspects to this individual named Ebed-Melech. First, we know he is from Ethiopia, and while some will presume to say he was not a Jewish male, I would argue that this would be too quick of a presumption.

If one goes back approximately four hundred years in time, to 1 Kings 10 and 2 Chronicles 9 in Scripture, we find a unique yet brief encounter between the Queen of Sheba and King Solomon. We all know how much of a "ladies' man" King Solomon was, and so the question must be asked – Was Queen Makeda, whose name many believe her name to be,[80] one of the women who was either a wife or a concubine of Solomon? If so, then the legends of this encounter include the queen returning to Sheba (modern-day Ethiopia) with a child of Solomon and the continuation of a Jewish legacy in Africa that began with Moses' wife Zipporah.[81]

Therefore, there is a good possibility that Ebed-Melech was at least Jewish, if not a descendant of Queen Makeda and King Solomon. Yet, he allowed himself to be a servant in the palace and to become a eunuch and to be present for Jeremiah when no one else was. Robin Gallaher Branch describes him well when she uses phrases such as "showing honor in chaos"

---

[79] An excellent summary of the Biblical definition of "mire," along with Scriptural references, can be found at the following link -- **https://bibledictionarytoday.com/words/mire/**. Accessed on 16 June 2025.

[80] Megan Sauter, "Who Is the Queen of Sheba in the Bible?: Investigating the Queen of Sheba and Her Kingdom," *Biblical Archaeology Society* (27 August 2024); available online at **https://www.biblicalarchaeology.org/daily/ancient-cultures/ancient-near-eastern-world/who-is-the-queen-of-sheba-in-the-bible/**; accessed 23 June 2025.

[81] Ibid. The reality of the Beta Israel/Falasha roots of Ethiopian Jewry is a fascinating study. A quick article on the subject was written by Ibraham Omir, "Evidence Mounts of Ancient Jewish Roots Beta Israel Ethiopian Jewry(16 June 2015); available online at **https://geneticliteracyproject.org/2015/06/16/evidence-mounts-of-ancient-jewish-roots-of-beta-israel-ethiopian-jewry/**; accessed 23 June 2025. A book that could prove interesting is Tudor Parfitt's *Journey to the Vanished City: The Search for a Lost Tribe of Israel* (New York: Knopf Doubleday Publishing Group, 2000).

and exhibiting "command appearance."[82] For, indeed, and aside from Jeremiah, Ebed-Melech was the only individual in the palace to exhibit any demonstration or understanding of God's judgment and righteousness over Jerusalem.

Yes … it is often the stranger or the unexpected person who steps in to lift us out of the slough of despond as John Bunyan describes Help in *Pilgrim's Progress*. The person who keeps us going when all we want to do is give up the spiritual battle – they come along with dirty rags (v. 11-12) and rescue us from ourselves.

One of the most challenging experiences of my parents' ministry occurred in a small Baptist church in Deep East Texas. Daddy had to face the fact that he had heard God wrong in accepting the call to take this church, and mama could do nothing but, as the old Tammy Wynette song says, "Stand by Her Man."

Both of them recognized the mistake almost immediately. Honestly, mama never wanted to move there, but she allowed her beloved to make the decision. Nearly from the beginning, there were conflicts with members and deacons, including the fact that at least two of the five deacons had sheets hanging in the back of their closets and membership cards for the KKK in their wallets.

Life did not get easier for my parents when their daughter (ME), who lived in a town not far away from my parents, refused to date the son of one of the KKK deacons, and mama refused to go walking at night with the wives of the racists. Daddy sought to work around the deacons and minister to those who wanted to overcome their racist legacy.

One of the KKK deacons fell ill with a strange illness and was unable to serve as a deacon any longer. The church began to attract new members who heard about the new pastor, who was not like their previous pastors. The young people started to grow in their relationship with Jesus. However, there was still the undercurrent of racism that was just beneath the surface, which seemingly was impossible to overcome.

Shortly before I began seminary in the fall of 1993, I went with my parents on a vacation to Mississippi – a vacation that included daddy preaching at a church that was considering him as a pastor. We all returned from the vacation on a Wednesday night, and daddy was preparing his devotion for the

---

[82] Robbin Gallaher Branch, "Ebedmelech—A Remarkable Figure in Jerusalem's Final Days," *Biblical Archaeology Society* (24 December 2024); available online at **https://www.biblicalarchaeology.org/daily/people-cultures-in-the-bible/people-in-the-bible/ebedmelech/**; accessed 23 June 2025.

service when one of the "good deacons" called to tell him what had happened that Sunday.

The remaining KKK deacon had arranged for a special business meeting on Sunday night and packed the pews with members who had not been there in months or even years – including the other KKK deacon and his family, who was soon to die. Long story short – daddy was fired in a falsely called business meeting without the pastor being present to answer questions or complaints. It was an emotional blow for my dad that almost crippled him in ways that I had never seen before.

Daddy was without a church for about ten weeks when a church in South Louisiana called him to be their pastor. It was a place that allowed him to heal, and mama met one of the two best friends of her life. It was a wonderful church for them and I am so grateful for the people at this Baptist church who fed them fried turkey and lots of beignets.

However, and before they moved to Louisiana, mama told me how she found daddy crying on the floor in the living room of the parsonage in the middle of the night (as daddy forced the church to let them live there rent-free until they found a new church – as the dismissal was a violation of their constitution). He was weeping. He was wailing. Mama described it as almost moaning in pain, and all she could do was hold him until he stopped. But … that was what he needed from her.

Mama was daddy's Ebed-Melech that night as she lifted him up when he was in his cistern of regret and remorse. She held him and reminded him that he was her knight, her rescuer, her hero. I ended up writing a short story about this event for their Christmas present that year, as I had no money for presents. As they read the pages based on the brief account of what mama told me, daddy once again cried, but this time, they were happy tears.

Happy tears because he knew he would always have an Ebed-Melech with him and that even in the darkest spiritual moments of his life, he would never be alone, and he could continue the battle. And … he did until 4 July 2000, when in the middle of the night an aneurysm burst and he went home. However, he managed to make it to mama so she could hold his hand one final time.

Questions for Individual or Group Study

1.   Without giving in to the tendency to give a "Sunday School Answer," what is your human response to the idea – **Spiritual warfare is about never changing God's message even after experiencing your own personal "well experience" … sometimes even from your own friends, family, and people closest to you.**

2.   Who is your "human" source for biblical truth and information? Why do you consider this person or group reliable? Is it because they are influential or have connections to someone important? Is that a good enough reason for them to be considered trustworthy?

3.   Have you ever found yourself at the bottom of a spiritual pit/well/cistern? Do you know what caused you to be thrown in the pit? What was your initial response? What was your spiritual response? Did you feel alone even if you were not really alone? Why or why not? How did you find your way out of the pit, or are you still there?

4.   Who is your Ebed-Melech when you are in the pit? Have you ever been an Ebed-Melech for someone? Have you ever expressed to this individual what they mean to your spiritual and emotional life? Why or why not?

14

Spiritual Warfare Is Often About Finding Hope in the Chaos
(Lamentations 3:1-66)

Spiritual warfare is often the most lonely experience on the face of the earth because it is defined by silence and isolation from God Himself. How one finds God again is the answer to the hope and spiritual warfare question.

Yes, I wrote the phrase "most lonely" instead of loneliest and I did it on purpose. Loneliest is simply an adjective of the word, while being most lonely is, from my perspective, a state of existence that goes beyond a simple definition. It is a state of existence in which one can be surrounded by people but feel absolutely isolated from everyone. It is a state of existence where an individual can belong but not belong at the same time (and if you have ever been there, you know what I mean). It is a state of existence where one is searching for God, but cannot find the Father, for he appears to have gone silent or even be missing when one needs him most.

At one time, I did not understand the idea of God's silence, but I was much younger then and much more naïve than I am now. Indeed, the concept of God being silent to his children was a foreign concept to me. So … when the pastor's wife of my seminary church (Wedgwood Baptist in Fort Worth, Texas) shared her testimony of experiencing months and perhaps even years of not hearing from God, I was confused. How could this godly woman who influenced and impacted so many struggle to hear God's voice? Today … I do understand it and the reality of straining to hear God's voice, but only hearing the void of emptiness still fills me with dread and terror.

I believe I first went through "the silence" the year after my daddy died. The loss of Jack Downey in my life took me to a level of grief that I could not express or imagine. I was a robot that only functioned at best. I ate. I tried to sleep. I went to church on Sundays. I read my Bible. I continued my work as a missionary to the Jewish people. But … I was on autopilot. They were functions because I could not hear God, and I definitely could not feel God in my life. My grief was overwhelming me to the point that I had lost my daddy, my best friend, and the man who showed me the way to God the Father.

C. S. Lewis, in his work *A Grief Observed*, written after the loss of his wife Joy Gresham Davidman, expresses it so well when he wrote: *"God has not been trying an experiment on my faith or love in order to find out their quality. He knew it already. It was I who didn't. In this trial[,] He makes us occupy the dock, the witness box, and the bench all at once.*

He always knew that my temple was a house of cards. His only way of making me realize the fact was to knock it down."

I had to come to the point of desperation to hear God's voice again – a desperation borne out of the truth – that I had made my beloved daddy an idol in order for God to begin talking to me again. I had to put God before my family, myself, and anything else that might obstruct my relationship with him. His way of getting my attention was to be silent – a silence that still terrifies me – because it has not been the only time he has been forced to use this tactic on me.

In this passage from Lamentations, Jeremiah also struggles with God's silence. I dare not presume to wonder why God is being silent towards the prophet at this time, but he was quiet, and it was such a burden to this man of God. For while being thrown down a well/cistern was bad and being told he would never marry or be a father was difficult, the silence of God while surrounded by the debris of Jerusalem apparently was more than the prophet could bear. Indeed, God's silence appears to be the greatest spiritual battle we must fight as well as the greatest spiritual discipline we must learn…

Jeremiah's Prayer of Confusion and Pain (3:1-66)

It is impossible to fairly cover the sixty-six verses of Jeremiah's prayer of lament, in chapter three, that came forth from his heart after the fall of Jerusalem to the Babylonians in 586 BC/BCE. Even today, the Jewish people read the laments of Jeremiah in commemoration of Tisha B'Av (ninth of Av) – the day of remembrance for the destruction of both the First and Second Temples.[83] Interestingly, the ninth of Av has been a very difficult day in Jewish history, as is recorded in the Mishnah (Oral Torah/Talmud):

> On the Ninth of Av it was decreed upon our ancestors that they would all die in the wilderness and not enter Eretz Yisrael; and the Temple was destroyed the first time, in the days of Nebuchadnezzar, and the second time, by the Romans; and Beitar was captured; and the city of Jerusalem was plowed, as a sign that it would never be rebuilt. Not only

---

[83] "About This Text – Lamentations," Available online at **https://www.sefaria.org/Lamentations?tab=contents**; accessed 28 June 2025. Sefaria is an online database to 3,000+ Jewish texts and is not associated with Messianic Judaism or Christian thought.

does one fast on the Ninth of Av, but from when the month of Av begins, one decreases acts of rejoicing.[84]

And while in Lamentations, we do find great cause to grieve, we also see moments of hope and slivers of sunlight, as will be noted in chapter 3. This is something that the Jewish people miss … even today. However, too many Christians immediately go to the faithfulness of God that is new every morning (3:23) without considering the process of recognizing this truth through nights of loss and grief. Balance is necessary, and when it is found, the spiritual battle can be overcome.

This balance begins by not skipping to verses 21-26 without going through the painful realities that Jeremiah experienced – especially those beginning in verse 1 through verse 18. Jeremiah saw affliction (v. 1), experienced physical pain (v. 3-4), lived through hardships that seem inescapable (v. 5-7, 9-11), caused the prophet to face derision and bitterness (v. 14-15), and forced him to live a life absent of peace and hope (v. 16-17). However, it is the words of verse 8 that most exemplify the why and how of the depth of battle that Jeremiah must have both faced and feared daily – God's silence. Jeremiah laments the reality of this silence when he writes, "Also when I cry and shout, he shuts out my prayer." The word for "shuts" is the Hebrew word shava, which conveys the idea of being free and crying out for help. Additionally, Jeremiah uses the Piel verb, which is an intensive way of expressing emotions. So … Jeremiah is intensely, gutturally shouting out to God – but there is only silence from the King of the Universe. Indeed, this is the essence of this greatest battle – utter spiritual loneliness, especially when you feel like God is refusing to hear and choosing not to listen to your prayers. The isolation is beyond terrifying. Yet … I would argue that it is perhaps something we all need to go through for a time so that we can truly appreciate fellowship with God and the necessity of never taking it for granted again.

Never taking the fellowship of God granted again begins by acknowledging two key words in verses 19-27 (yes, we are allowed to hold onto the cheerful verses in this tough chapter). The first is remember(ing) or *zachor* in Hebrew and good (*tob*). We must **remember** the difficult times for what they were meant to teach us and then acknowledge one unchallengeable fact – God is good (v. 25). It is also good that we wait for him, and we should bear his yoke on our lives (v. 26-27). This is the hope of God's faithfulness (v. 23) and

---

[84] Mishnah Ta'anit 4.6, Available online at **https://www.sefaria.org/Mishnah_Ta'anit.4.6?lang=bi&with=all&lang2=en**; accessed 28 June 2025. The capture of Beitar occurred during the Bar Kokhba Rebellion (AD/CE 132-135). However, it should be noted that Jerusalem has been rebuilt as promised in Ezekiel.

what Jesus reminded the people when he told them to take his yoke upon them in Matt. 11:28-30.

However, and in taking on God's yoke, we also take on the responsibility of submitting to actions that, while not always pleasant, are for our human/selfish edification. Here are three actions that Jesus both experienced and taught in his earthly ministry – (1) allowing yourself to be "filled with reproach" by being slapped (v. 30), and the teaching of Jesus in Matt. 5:39; (2) knowing that if one mourns then they shall also be comforted (v. 32) and the Beatitude promise of Matt. 5:4; and (3) never be guilty of robbing someone else – even if we must suffer, whether it be personally or in the eyes of others (v-35-36; cf. Matthew 15:1-9; Mark 7:1-13).

Jeremiah closes out this third lament (which interestingly is an acrostic of the Hebrew alphabet) much like David did with many of his lament psalms – by acknowledging the greatness of God and thanking Jehovah for his deliverance (v. 55-66). Deliverance is a word that we do not consider enough ... in my opinion. We thank God for safety, security, and salvation, but do we thank him for delivering us from things we don't deserve or perhaps even things we do deserve? I wonder.

Yet, Jeremiah spent multiple verses praising and thanking God for deliverance. There are multiple reasons why Jeremiah thanked God in this passage, including having his life redeemed (v. 58), having his oppression seen (v. 59), and not only stopping the plans of Jeremiah's enemies but also destroying them (v. 60-66). However, the greatest deliverance that Jeremiah experienced is found in verses 55-57, and that is when God heard his voice from the lowest pit and said the most wonderful words anyone can hear, "Fear not."

Hearing Jehovah (for this is the word in Hebrew that Jeremiah called out) tell him to no longer fear must have been the greatest sound (words) in his life. The same is true for us as well. For we live in a fearful world – not only because of the tumultuous nature of political and global events, but also because our spiritual environment is often unstable. Fear is not what we long to hear as we fight battles we never anticipated fighting when we first asked Jesus to save our souls, but ones we must fight daily as a part of our spiritual growth and our sanctification. And knowing that God hears our voice, even when there are periods when we do wonder if he is listening, is a relief beyond imagination and hope.

As I close this chapter, I am going to share a part of my mama's life that I would not be sharing if my mama were still here. I shared briefly in chapter five that my grandmother (mama's mother) was an unkind woman and that her method of discipline was to be silent towards my sweet mama. Yet, it was not simply speaking to mama that my grandmother utilized as discipline when she was angry. Mama shared with us that, as she grew older, silence was a normal fact of life in their home.

There was little talking (if at all) around the dinner table. If grandpa wanted to listen to the St. Louis Cardinals on the radio, he had to go outside or into a back room to listen to his favorite sport. There were no words of praise for her daughter growing up, and the idea of hearing "I love you" from the woman was something that rarely, if ever, came out of her mouth.

If you could look back at pictures of my grandmother, you would rarely see a smile on her face, and any laughter or joy for my mama growing up came only from the hugs and smiles of Grandpa Butler. It was only when Barbara Butler became Barbara Downey that she discovered families talked, joked, and laughed around the dinner table. It was only then that she discovered that families can be noisy, loud, and argumentative, yet still love each other at the end of the day. She clung to Gramma Downey (her mother-in-law) for it was only then that she discovered what a mama truly could be.

Mama worked diligently to be the best wife and mother for her husband and children. In fact, my daddy was a spoiled man in many ways because he rescued her, and she wanted him to know that she adored him. My sister and I constantly heard the words, "I love you," and "You are so special," because she never wanted us to doubt our worth and value in her eyes. My niece, her granddaughter, was the apple of her eye and could do little wrong – even during her bratty stage – because she wanted everyone to know how special her grandbaby was in her life. And, yes, our home was noisy and loud, and even when we argued, we knew we were loved.

For mama was terrified of silence. She could not abide a quiet room. Silence brought her back to her childhood, her mother, and her greatest fears. And, so, when I watched mama's last few days slip by, I watched as she listened for and began to hear the voice of God telling her to come on home. I could not listen to it, but I watched her face as she began to hear his voice and saw her eyes light up with a light that cannot be described. She was hearing the echoes of sounds that we cannot hear in this world, for it is a fallen world – much like it is described in C. S. Lewis' *Out of the Silent Planet* – but my sweet mama heard the voice of God. And so, when I told mama at 8:29 a.m. on June 20, 2020, it was okay to go home, she stopped hearing my voice and heard clearly the voice of God saying, "Welcome Home," for her spiritual warfare was finally over.

Questions for Individual or Group Study

1.   Without giving in to the tendency to give a "Sunday School Answer," what is your human response to the idea – **Spiritual warfare is often the most lonely experience on the face of the earth because it is defined by silence**

and isolation from God Himself. How one finds God again is the answer to the hope and spiritual warfare question.

2.   Have you ever gone through a time when you felt as if your prayers were bouncing off the ceiling and never reaching Heaven? Can you identify with the pain of Lamentations 3:8? What brought you through that moment? If you are still in the moment, what are you doing to get through this loneliness? How would you help someone else going through it?

3.   Is taking on the yoke of God an uncomfortable thought for you? Losing a part of your freedom, your individuality, to gain a more personal relationship with God – is it really worth it? Did any of those examples from Lamentations 3 and the teachings of Jesus strike a chord and/or nerve with you? Which ones? Why?

4.   My mother's greatest fear was silence. What is your greatest fear in life and does it translate over into your relationship with God? If so, how and why does it do so? How can you give over your fear to God as you fight this greatest spiritual battle? Are you willing to let it go?

Some Concluding Thoughts:
A Most Difficult Book?

(Including Some Final Thoughts from Lamentations 5:1-22)

I have to be honest with you that this has been one of the most difficult writing exercises I have ever undertaken in my life. I have written two master's theses and one PhD dissertation, but none of them has been as difficult as this book. And before you think I am exaggerating, I promise you I am not.

As I wrote every chapter, I felt as if I were undergoing the spiritual warfare about which I was writing. The testing and the skirmishes were real. I struggled at times to finish every chapter because I dreaded going on to the next chapter. I was afraid of what I might face next.

Whether it was a personal spiritual battle I was experiencing or the events that were occurring in the Middle East between Israel and Hamas or Israel and Iran, the events that I was confronting seemed to mirror the words I was writing on my laptop. It was at times more than I could bear. I felt so inadequate to write this book, even though I knew that God was telling me to write it. How could I seek to help you when I was unable to help myself?

And then I approached the Jeremiah section with even more trepidation than I thought possible – I found myself literally nauseous at times, and I wondered if I would find myself at the bottom of a well before this book was finished. Again … I am not exaggerating!

I found myself crying and praying in the bathtub more often than I would like to admit – and please tell me that I am not the only one who prays while showering/bathing. It was then that I realized it was not only about the spiritual weaknesses in my life that God was helping me overcome, but also that I was being burdened by what I saw in the world today. And much like Jeremiah wrote in Lamentations 5, he struggled to understand why he had to be punished for the sins of others. And it was then that I realized I was fighting discontent over the same issue.

Why is it that I am being punished for the sins of others? Why do I have to be held back because others are living a life of sin that I am not committing? Why cannot I be exempt from the punishment that others are experiencing? Why? Why? Why?

Jeremiah was not like Daniel or Ezra – who prayed on behalf of the nation of Israel and acknowledged national sin even though they were not guilty. Jeremiah was mad and 5:19-22 shows it:

Thou, O Lord, remainest forever; thy throne from generation to generation.

> Wherefore dost thou forget us forever, and forsake us so long time? Turn thou us unto thee, O Lord, and we shall be turned; renew our days as of old. But thou hast utterly rejected us; thou art very wroth against us.

Now … the King James, while beautiful and passionate in its Shakespearean tone, might not convey what we seek to share today. However, the essence is basically – God is angry, and Jeremiah wondered if he would ever get over being mad at Israel (and consequently, Jeremiah would be punished along with the rest of the people)?

However, and this may be the final spiritual warfare lesson of the book, we need to pray corporately for the sins of our nation. I know that people often recite 2 Chronicles 7:14 as a panacea, but aside from being taken out of context, we need to look more closely at Daniel's prayer for Israel (9:1-19), along with Ezra's prayer (9:5-15), to show us what a battle prayer should be. Yes … we grow weary like Jeremiah, but we must never pray **about** someone or a people but pray **for** them **and include** ourselves in an acknowledgement of sins.

Definitely a hard thing to do, but something I had to learn about myself (once again) in the process of finishing this book. And something I will probably have to learn again and again and again.

As I close with the final words on this most difficult book, I pray that you now realize that demons are not under every rock for us to battle, but that spiritual warfare is a part of our spiritual discipline, our maturation as believers in Messiah Jesus. Fight the battle. Grow in your walk with God. We need more warriors in the days to come because the struggle is coming hard and fierce, and it will only grow harder. Fight…

www.ingramcontent.com/pod-product-compliance
Lightning Source LLC
Chambersburg PA
CBHW072202090426
42740CB00012B/2356